Junior Skill Builders

SPELLING
in
15 Minutes a Day

LearningExpress®

NEW YORK

Published in the United States by LearningExpress, LLC, New York.

Library of Congress Control Number: 2009927186

A copy of this title is on file with the Library of Congress.

ISBN: 978-1-57685-690-1

Printed in the United States of America

9 8 7 6 5 4 3 2

For more information or to place an order, contact LearningExpress at:
  2 Rector Street
  26th Floor
  New York, NY 10006

Or visit us at:
  www.learnatest.com

C O N T E N T S

 INTRODUCTION

SPELLING CAN BE tricky. The English language is filled with foreign phrases, technical terms, homonyms, and words that don't seem to make any sense at all. It is easy to be tripped up by the many rules—and exceptions to the rules—that go along with them. If you have picked up this book, chances are you think your spelling could use some improvement. And if you are a less-than-stellar speller, it can be difficult to know how to begin to improve your spelling. Memorizing spelling lists probably seems a bit daunting, not to mention boring.

What's more, with the advent of spell-check programs, you might think that being a good speller isn't even all that important anymore. After all, you can rely on technology to catch your errors, right? Not necessarily. Spell-check programs aren't always reliable. Many errors can go undetected, especially the incorrect use of homonyms, many foreign words, and new or technical terms that haven't made it into the spell-check dictionary. If you really want to ensure accuracy, you must learn to spell properly.

Relying on spell-check programs or thinking that no one will notice or care if you spell words incorrectly can cause plenty of problems. This is especially true in the case of formal writing. Although much of our correspondence these days is fairly casual, through e-mail and text messages, there is still a place for formal writing in our society. Throughout your life, you will be required to write essays, applications, letters, resumes, business memos, reports, and other correspondence. In addition, formal e-mails for school and business require proper spelling. Making spelling errors on your college applications, for example, could cost you a coveted spot at your first-choice school. Later, mistakes on your resume could cost you a job offer.

It isn't just the big spelling errors that can cause problems for you. The repeated misspelling of simple words in your e-mails, letters, reports, or anything else that you write in your daily life can make you appear careless, lazy, and not very intelligent. Luckily, these spelling mistakes are easily corrected. Most spelling mistakes are common, with a few dozen of them accounting for the majority of all errors. If you learn these common errors and how to correct and avoid them, your spelling ability will increase dramatically. That is what this book will help you to do.

This book will not attempt to have you memorize list after list of words. Yes, there are several lists included in this book that you should spend time reading and absorbing. However, the lessons in this book are designed to teach you the reasons why words are spelled the way they are—and, perhaps more importantly, why they are *not* spelled the way you may think they are—with the hope that by gaining that type of understanding, you will improve your spelling ability. In addition, the book is filled with tips, tricks, and rules you can follow to improve your spelling every day.

If you work through each lesson, you will learn easy ways to become a better speller. And the emphasis here is on *easy*. Each lesson is designed to take you 15 minutes to complete. To accomplish this, any spelling complexities have been broken down into manageable rules and tips, making each lesson very focused and specific.

The best way to get started using this book is to take the pretest that follows. Complete each question and then check your work in the answer key. Once you've done this, you will have a good idea of the areas in which you have the most room for improvement. After you finish all the lessons in the book, take the time to complete the posttest. If you've dedicated the time to the pursuit of becoming a better speller, you're sure to do better on the posttest than you did on the pretest.

So, let's get started. Grab a pencil and take your time on the pretest. Good luck!

PRETEST

THIS BOOK STARTS with a pretest, to give you an idea of where your spelling strengths and weaknesses lie. The pretest consists of 30 questions designed to assess your knowledge of the major spelling concepts and rules that are covered in this book. If you don't know an answer to a particular question, resist the urge to guess. This test is designed to measure what you know. If you don't know a particular answer, that gives you a pretty good indication that you should pay attention to the lesson covering that concept!

Check your work when you're done by looking at the answers on page 6.

Write out each word, using hyphens to divide it by its syllables.

1. comment

2. unreachable

3. euphoric

4. lavish

5. August

Match the words with their correct meanings.

6. eligible

7. occupy

8. anecdote

9. malaise

10. vendetta

11. boisterous

a. loud

b. qualified to participate

c. a short account of an interesting or humorous incident

d. a grudge or feud characterized by acts of retaliation

e. a feeling of mental unease or discomfort

f. to take up a place or space

Choose the correct word to complete each sentence.

12. The *two / too* girls were shopping for prom dresses.

13. She couldn't *bear / bare* to see her sister cry.

14. Brianne was thrilled that she *passed / past* her math exam.

15. Tom doesn't like the *coarse / course* texture of cornbread.

16. I *ensured / assured* Becky that her new hairstyle was attractive.

17. She selected heavy stock for her *stationery / stationary*.

Circle the correct form of *lay / lie* in each sentence.

18. Evan found his textbook *laying / lying* under his bed.

19. Parker had *laid / lain* awake for 10 minutes before getting out of bed.

Circle the correct form of *sit / set* in each sentence.

20. *Setting / Sitting* on the hammock is very enjoyable.

21. Mom asked me to *set / sit* the table for dinner.

Circle the italicized word that is spelled correctly.

22. My dad's boss gave him an increase in his annual *salery / salary*.

23. Amber filled her award speech with *clichés / chlishés*.

24. It was unfortunate that Robbie didn't pass *nineth / ninth* grade.

25. *Febuary / February* is Black History Month.

Correctly spell the plural forms of the following words.

26. goose

27. book

28. self

29. truck

30. tornado

ANSWERS

1. com-ment (Lesson 3)
2. un-reach-a-ble (Lesson 3)
3. eu-phor-ic (Lesson 3)
4. lav-ish (Lesson 3)
5. Aug-ust (Lesson 3)
6. b. (Lesson 4)
7. f. (Lesson 4)
8. c. (Lesson 4)
9. e. (Lesson 4)
10. d. (Lesson 4)
11. a. (Lesson 4)
12. The *two* girls were shopping for prom dresses. (Lesson 25)
13. She couldn't *bear* to see her sister cry. (Lesson 25)
14. Brianne was thrilled that she *passed* her math exam. (Lesson 25)
15. Tom doesn't like the *coarse* texture of cornbread. (Lesson 25)
16. I *assured* Becky that her new hairstyle was attractive. (Lesson 25)
17. She selected heavy stock for her *stationery*. (Lesson 25)
18. Evan found his textbook *lying* under his bed. (Lesson 27)
19. Parker had *lain* awake for 10 minutes before getting out of bed. (Lesson 27)
20. *Sitting* on the hammock is very enjoyable. (Lesson 27)
21. Mom asked me to *set* the table for dinner. (Lesson 27)
22. My dad's boss gave him an increase in his annual *salary*. (Lesson 28)
23. Amber filled her award speech with *clichés*. (Lesson 30)
24. It was unfortunate that Robbie didn't pass *ninth* grade. (Lesson 23)
25. *February* is Black History Month. (Lesson 26)
26. geese (Lesson 21)
27. books (Lesson 20)
28. selves (Lesson 20)
29. trucks (Lesson 20)
30. tornadoes (Lesson 20)

S E C T I O N 1

spelling strategies

EMPLOYING A FEW key strategies will shorten the amount of time it takes for you to become a better speller. Think about the strategies outlined in this section as you would think about any other plan; they are steps for you to take to reach your ultimate goal. In this case, your goal is to boost your spelling ability. Following the tips, tricks, and other tactics in this section will help you to do just that!

how to become a better speller

*When our spelling is perfect, it's invisible. But when
it's flawed, it prompts strong negative associations.*
—MARILYN VOS SAVANT (1946–)
AMERICAN MAGAZINE COLUMNIST

In this first lesson, we'll cover some of the tactics that you can employ to reinforce
what you learn in each of the lessons in this book.

THE FIRST STEP to becoming a better speller is not to despair over your current spelling ability. You may think you are a terrible speller, but that doesn't
mean you will always be a terrible speller. Good spellers are not born; they are
made through instruction and practice. So, instead of worrying about being a
less-than-stellar speller, put your energies toward learning a few tips and tricks
that will vastly improve your spelling skills.

Each lesson in this book will cover a specific tip, trick, or rule that when
learned and applied will set you on your way toward better spelling. Before you
get started, take some time to read through the guidelines here for how to reinforce those tips, tricks, and rules.

USE FLASH CARDS

At first, you might feel silly using flash cards, but once you notice that you are no longer making careless spelling mistakes, chances are you won't mind being a bit silly. Flash cards are easy and convenient to use. All you need to create them is a pack of index cards or scraps of paper and a pen. Here are some ways in which you can use flash cards to your advantage:

- On the front of each card, write a word you want to learn. Leave out a key letter. Write the complete word on the back. Quiz yourself by trying to fill in the blank correctly.
- Write a complete word on one side of each card. On the other side, write the definition(s) of the word. Quiz yourself by reading the word and trying to state the definition(s). Conversely, you can read the definition(s) and try to identify the word.
- Instead of trying to learn hundreds of words, use flash cards to learn roots, prefixes, and suffixes.

You could also have a friend quiz you. Have someone say a word from your deck of flash cards and then try to spell that word, either out loud or on a separate sheet of paper.

MAKE A PERSONALIZED SPELLING LIST

Once you've completed the lessons in this book, there will probably still be certain words that trip you up. However, if you've read the lessons carefully and completed the practice exercises, you will have a firmer grasp on your spelling errors. In other words, by learning the whys and hows of spelling, you'll be more aware of words that you typically spell incorrectly. Make a list of those words and try to use them in your writing as often as possible. This may seem like an odd instruction: If the words are tricky, shouldn't you just avoid them? Well, no. If you have a hard time spelling a word, forcing yourself to use it—correctly— as often as possible, will reinforce the word in your mind.

Maybe you've misspelled *definitely* for as long as you can remember, writing it as *definately*. Since that incorrect spelling has become ingrained, you might have trouble imagining the word spelled differently. But once you become aware of your error, and come to understand the meaning of the root *finite*, the spelling will make sense to you (see Lesson 5 for more on word roots). It might take time for that new understanding to stick, though. That's where practice becomes essential. Using the correct spelling of *definitely* as frequently as you can will ensure that it replaces the incorrect spelling in your mind for good.

READ, READ, AND READ SOME MORE

One of the easiest ways to improve your spelling ability is to read. The more you read, the more you will recognize words that are spelled properly. When you read, you will experience language. You will be exposed to new and different words and you will see them in action. Reading will allow you to understand tricky words in the context of others. All of this will reinforce your spelling skills.

Don't think, however, that you need to force yourself to read dry or dull texts. Read whatever you want to! Newspapers, graphic novels, short stories, magazines, blogs, and novels are all full of words that can expand your knowledge. If you read many different media, you will be exposed to many different types of words. So don't turn your nose up at the dry texts; just make sure you read other things, too!

When you read, you might want to try keeping a dictionary handy. Then, when you come across a word that you don't know, you can look it up right away. Chances are, you'll find yourself reading words that you've used when speaking but haven't known how they were spelled. Take a look at Lesson 4 for more information on using the dictionary and understanding word meanings.

....

TIP: Your school or local library is filled with books, magazines, and journals that can help you improve your spelling. Not only can you borrow books and periodicals from the library but most libraries offer a variety of self-improvement, computer, hobby, and other courses free of charge. The next time you are at the library, ask for a copy of its most recent newsletter, bulletin, or calendar of events.

....

PLAY WORD GAMES

Gather some family members or friends to play word games like Scrabble® or Boggle®. Or, if you prefer a more solitary pursuit, do crossword puzzles or jumbles. Most daily newspapers have crossword puzzles and many of them also have jumbles. You can also purchase books dedicated to word games, or visit websites that feature jumbles and crossword puzzles.

When you are online, why not sign up for *Word of the Day* e-mails? These will enhance your vocabulary and increase your familiarity with the spelling of various words. Many sites offer this type of service, including www.dictionary.com.

TURN OFF YOUR SPELL-CHECK FUNCTION

If you are a subpar speller, the notion of turning off your spell-check function may seem scary. After all, you rely on your spell-check to catch your mistakes, right? Well, that may not be the best thing to do. First, spell-check tools aren't all that reliable. If you spell a word correctly, but use it incorrectly (in the case of homonyms, for example), your spell-check will not alert you to the error. Second, spell-check tools usually make changes automatically, so quickly that you may not even notice the change has been made. In this way, the spell-check tool actually reinforces your spelling errors. Not what you want to do when you are attempting to improve your ability!

Turning off your spell-check function will force you to proofread your writing very carefully. As you do, if you are unsure of how to spell a word, you can look it up in the dictionary immediately, which will help you learn correct spelling. This may take a little more time than you are used to spending on your writing, but there will be many benefits. Taking charge of your spelling in everything you write will make you a more confident and competent speller.

ASK FOR HELP

If you really want to improve your spelling, don't be shy. Tell your parents, teachers, employers, and friends that you are attempting to become a better speller. Then, ask them to point out any spelling errors you make in your e-mails, letters, or papers. If you know someone who is a particularly good speller or apt proofreader, ask him or her to proofread for a period of time everything that you write, or at least your very important papers or letters! Having another person's eyes review your material may help pinpoint spelling errors that you never knew you were making.

Other keys to becoming a better speller are outlined in the following lessons in this section: Use mnemonics, practice proper pronunciation, and pay attention to word meanings. Furthermore, it goes without saying that you should read all of the lessons in this book and spend the time to complete the practice exercises. In spelling, practice really does make perfect!

PRACTICE

How many words can you create from these letters?

1. RNEIGW

2. LSYFHA

3. ERSUSI

4. SNIGEB

5. OTSRHF

ANSWERS

If you don't know what all of the words mean, take this opportunity to look them up in your dictionary.

1. There are 21 possible words.

erg	reign	win
gen	rein	wine
gin	rig	wing
grew	ring	winger
grin	weir	wire
ire	wen	wren
new	wig	wring

2. There are 22 possible words.

ash	fly	lay
ashy	half	lays
fay	has	say
fays	hay	shay
flash	hays	shy
flashy	las	slay
flay	lash	sly
flays		

3. There are 25 possible words.

ire	ruse	suer
ires	ruses	suers
issue	sir	sues
issuer	sire	sure
res	sires	use
rise	sirs	user
rises	sis	users
rue	sue	uses
rues		

4. There are 25 possible words.

beg	binge	ins
begin	binges	nib
begins	bins	nibs
begs	gen	sign
being	gibe	sin
beings	gibes	sine
bes	gin	sing
big	gins	singe
bin		

5. There are 23 possible words.

for	froths	rots
fort	host	short
forth	hot	shot
forts	hots	soft
fro	oft	sort
frosh	ors	sot
frost	rho	tor
froth	rot	

mnemonics

Memory is the mother of all wisdom.
—AESCHYLUS (525–456 B.C.)
GREEK PLAYWRIGHT

In this lesson, you will learn about mnemonics—memory aids to help you become a better speller.

TALK ABOUT A tricky word! *Mnemonic* might be a hard word to spell, but it is a simple concept. Meaning *memory aid*, mnemonics can be handy for helping you remember spelling rules, or how to spell particularly difficult words. They are typically phrases or rhymes that are used to make memorization easier. The idea behind mnemonics is that people remember best when more than one function of the brain is used to process information.

Simple mnemonics can be created from rhymes, tunes, or acronyms. You may recall the acronym *Roy G. Biv*, the grade school mnemonic used when learning the colors of the spectrum (red, orange, yellow, green, blue, indigo, violet). Mental pictures and stories are also useful mnemonics.

Quite a few mnemonics apply to spelling. Here are some of the most common ones:

- *i* before *e*, except after *c*.

This clever rhyme is one of the best-known mnemonics. It means that in most words that have the letters *i* and *c* grouped together, the *i* will come before the *e*, except in words where there is a *c* immediately before this combination. For example, in the word *niece,* the *i* comes before the *e,* and in the word *receipt,* the *e* comes before the *i* because the combination is preceded by a *c.*

For more on *ie* and *ei* combinations, including exceptions to the rule, see Lesson 12.

- When two vowels go walking, the first one does the talking.

Let's break down the rhyme to fully understand it. *When two vowels go walking* refers to a two-vowel combination in a word. For example, abst*ai*n, fl*ea*, f*oe*, and tr*ue*. *The first one does the talking* means that in the two-vowel combinations, only the first vowel is pronounced and the second one is silent. In the case of our examples, you hear the long *a* in *abstain,* but not the *i.* In *flea,* you hear the long *e* but not the *a,* and in *foe* you hear the long *o* but not the *e.*

For more on vowel combinations, see Lesson 11.

- You *hear* with your *ear.*

This is an easy way to differentiate the words *hear* and *here.* If you remember the mnemonic, you'll remember that the word *ear* is in the word that means *to listen to.*

- *Desserts* have two sugars.

This one will help you avoid confusing *desert* (the sandy, arid land) with *dessert* (the sweet ending to a meal). *Sugars* then, refers to the *ss* in the word *dessert.*

- There is *a rat* in *separate.*

So often, the word *separate* is misspelled as *seperate.* Remember the rat to remember the correct spelling!

- The *principal* is my *pal.*

This mnemonic will help you distinguish between a pair of frequently confused homonyms. (Homonyms will be explained later, so don't worry if you're not sure what they are.) If you remember that the *principal* of your school is your *pal,* you will not confuse the *principal* of a school with the word *principle,* meaning *rule of action or conduct.*

You can devise mnemonics for any spelling rules or words you find particularly difficult. Here are some tips on creating mnemonics that will be easy to remember and, therefore, useful. (If you can't even remember your mnemonic, it won't help you to remember your spelling!)

- Use rhymes, rhythmic patterns, or tunes.
- Try humorous or odd sayings that will stick in your mind.
- Exaggerate features or images to make them vivid.
- Make your mnemonics personally meaningful.

PRACTICE

Using the mnemonics that we reviewed in this chapter, choose the correctly spelled version of the italicized words in the following sentences.

1. Angela went back for a second *piece* / *peice* of pizza.

2. Pete and Rory have been *freinds* / *friends* since they were seven years old.

3. We were instructed to cut against the *grain* / *grian*.

4. I didn't *here* / *hear* the doorbell when it rang.

5. Ashley was admired by her teachers because of her good moral *principals* / *principles*.

6. The recipe required me to whip the eggs *separately* / *seperately* from the other ingredients.

7. Grace asked her mother to make tiramisu for her birthday dinner *dessert* / *desert*.

8. The babysitter was *afraid* / *afriad* of the two pit bulls.

9. Julia was confused when she was called to the *principal's* / *principle's* office.

10. She almost *fianted* / *fainted* when walking down the hall.

ANSWERS

1. Angela went back for a second *piece* of pizza.
2. Pete and Rory have been *friends* since they were seven years old.
3. We were instructed to cut against the *grain*.
4. I didn't *hear* the doorbell when it rang.
5. Ashley was admired by her teachers because of her good moral *principles*.
6. The recipe required me to whip the eggs *separately* from the other ingredients.
7. Grace asked her mother to make tiramisu for her birthday dinner *dessert*.
8. The babysitter was *afraid* of the two pit bulls.
9. Julia was confused when she was called to the *principal's* office.
10. She almost *fainted* when walking down the hall.

pronunciation

Take care that you never spell a word wrong. Always before
you write a word, consider how it is spelled, and,
if you do not remember, turn to a dictionary.
It produces great praise to a lady to spell well.
—THOMAS JEFFERSON (1743–1826)
THIRD PRESIDENT OF THE UNITED STATES
TO HIS DAUGHTER MARTHA

Sounding out words can help you remember how to spell them. Learn how proper pronunciation and sounding out words can improve your spelling.

SLOPPY PRONUNCIATION IS one of the fastest routes to sloppy spelling. If you get in the habit of dropping syllables or letters from words when you speak, you may find yourself dropping them when you write. For example, you might write *innermural* when the correct spelling is *intramural*. If you run the first two syllables together rather than enunciating properly, you may erroneously translate the way you pronounce the word to the way you spell it. Another sloppy pronunciation that may result in sloppy spelling is saying *inneresting* instead of articulating *interesting*. Or, *frigerator* instead of *refrigerator*.

Similarly, many people tend to drop the final *g* sound when they say words ending in *-ing*. This habit can cause you to make some pretty silly errors, by failing to remember the *-g* at the end of the words you mispronounce.

Practicing correct pronunciation will help you to avoid sloppy spelling errors. When you speak, pay attention to what you are saying. Make an effort to enunciate properly and speak your words in the exact way they are meant to be pronounced. You will be amazed at how changing the way you pronounce your words can strengthen your spelling. Once you begin to enunciate more clearly, you will find that it becomes a habit. It's helpful to practice by sounding out every letter of certain words, in order to remember how to spell them. Sometimes exaggerating the pronunciation can help you remember the spelling.

Even if you enunciate well, many words can throw you off because they are not spelled as they are pronounced. If you didn't know how to spell the word *restaurant*, for example, based on pronunciation, you might think it should be written as *resterant*.

Here is a list of words that are commonly misspelled either because they are often mispronounced or because their pronunciation is quite different from the way they are spelled.

across	disastrous	mischievous
again	environment	narrator
allege	equipment	opportunity
always	extraordinary	outrageous
bargain	familiar	practically
basically	February	preferred
biscuit	gauge	privilege
business	generally	recognize
candidate	jewelry	restaurant
clothes	library	schedule
colonel	lightning	tyranny
congratulations	maneuver	undoubtedly
consistent	minuscule	valuable
desperate		

TIP: Two vowels written together often have the sound of a single vowel. This can lead to spelling errors. If you are familiar with a word through speaking, but not through writing or reading it, and you don't know how to spell it, you may be thrown off by a vowel combination. This is one reason why using your dictionary to look up any words that you don't know how to spell is a good habit to acquire.

USING THE DICTIONARY

You are probably familiar with the dictionary as a source for definitions. Chances are, you don't use the dictionary's pronunciation guides as frequently. If that is the case, then you might not be familiar with accent and diacritical marks. Not to worry! With a little instruction, you can become a pro at using your dictionary.

First, let's take a look at some of the basic features of a dictionary. For starters, all of the words in the dictionary are listed in alphabetical order. The two words at the top of each page are guide words, indicating the first and last words on the page. Looking at the guide words will let you easily locate the particular word you want to review.

Each word in a dictionary is written two ways: as it is correctly spelled (the entry word) and according to its pronunciation. The correct spelling entry needs little explanation. The second way the word is written can be confusing, however. When the entry is written according to its pronunciation, each sound in the word is marked with a symbol. Most consonants are readily recognizable, with the actual letters representing the sounds. But vowels can have multiple pronunciations, so they are marked differently. The marks for the vowel sounds are called diacritical marks. The beginning of your dictionary will usually give a key to these marks. Diacritical marks may vary from dictionary to dictionary, so you should take a look at the guide of any new dictionary that you use to make sure you know what each mark means.

....

TIP: What is a syllable? Using the dictionary, we can find the following definition:

Syllable: syl-la-ble—noun

1. An uninterrupted segment of speech consisting of a center of relatively great sonority with or without one or more accompanying sounds of relatively less sonority.
2. One or more written letters or characters representing more or less exactly such an element of speech.
3. The slightest portion or amount of speech or writing.

In other words, syllables are the individual spoken units of a word.

....

The phonetically spelled words are broken out into syllables and the accented syllables are marked as such. Accents are important because each word of two or more syllables has one syllable that is given more emphasis than the others. In the dictionary, that emphasis is shown by an accent mark ('). Some words have more than one syllable that is accented, with one heavier than the other. The heavier accent is called the primary accent and the other is the secondary accent. Here is what accented words would look like in a dictionary:

one accent:

meet' ing

play' er

two accents:

in' for ma' tion

GENERAL PRONUNCIATION GUIDE

The following pronunciation guide will show you how the main sounds in the English language are pronounced.

ă   *a* as in **a**pple

ā   *a* as in **a**ce

ä   *a* as in st**a**r

âr   *ar* as in c**are**

ə   *a* as in **a**bout, *e* as in th**e**, *i* as in penc**i**l, *o* as in bish**o**p, *u* as in s**u**pply

b   *b* as in **b**aby

ch   *ch* as in **ch**icken

d   *d* as in **d**og

ĕ   *e* as in b**e**t

ē   *e* as in compl**e**te, *y* as in hungr**y**

ər   *er* as in butt**er**, *ir* as in b**ir**d, *or* as in doct**or**, *ur* as in **ur**ge

f   *f* as in **f**ast, *ph* as in **ph**one

g   *g* as in **g**ood

h   *h* as in **h**at

ĭ   *i* as in h**i**m

îr   *ier* as in p**ier**, *ear* as in f**ear**

ī   *i* as in **i**ce

j   *j* as in **j**ob

k	*k* as in **k**id, *c* as in **c**ookie
l	*l* as in **l**ie, *le* as in beet**le**
m	*m* as in **m**an
n	*n* as in f**u**n
ŏ	*o* as in m**o**p
ō	*o* as in t**o**e
ô	*o* as in t**o**rn, *a* as in w**a**rm, *aw* as in **aw**kward
oi	*oi* as in n**oi**se, *oy* as in b**oy**
û	*oo* as in f**oo**t, *u* as in p**u**t
ow	*ou* as in **ou**t
p	*p* as in **p**in
r	*r* as in **r**eal
s	*s* as in me**s**s, *c* as in **c**ity
t	*t* as in **t**iny
th	*th* as in **th**e
<u>th</u>	*th* as in **th**in
ŭ	*u* as in r**u**n, *o* as in h**o**ney
ū	*u* as in **u**niform
ü	*oo* as in b**oo**t
yû	*u* as in **c**ure, **c**ute
v	*v* as in **v**isit
w	*w* as in **w**hy
z	*z* as in **z**ombie
zh	*si* as in vi**si**on, *ge* as in gara**ge**

. . . .

TIP: A good dictionary will include more than just definitions. When looking for a dictionary, make sure it includes the phonetic spelling of each word and a full pronunciation key at the beginning of the dictionary. The pronunciation key should include all of the pronunciation symbols used in the dictionary to represent the words phonetically. Once you have found a dictionary that meets your needs, take some time to review the pronunciation key and learn the symbols. You will then be well equipped to improve your spelling through improved pronunciation.

. . . .

SOUNDING WORDS OUT

There are two ways in which sounding words out can benefit you in your quest to become a better speller. The first is to sound out tricky words when you read them. If you are reading a newspaper article or a website and you notice a word that you are unfamiliar with or have never had occasion to spell, sound it out. Break the word into syllables, saying each one aloud as you read it. Once you have each of the syllables down, string them together and say the whole word, thinking about how the sound of the word and its spelling are related.

For example, if you were to read the word *tranquility* you would break it down into four syllables like this: *tran-quil-i-ty*. Say each syllable slowly, committing the spelling of each to memory. Then, when you put the syllables together, you will be able to spell the whole word.

The second technique for sounding words out is to exaggerate the way a word is spelled, or the way it sounds, or some part of the word. This technique is similar to the mnemonics that you learned about in Lesson 2. The English language has hundreds of words that are not spelled the way they sound, with silent letters and letter combinations that can mislead even the best spellers. Exaggerating these idiosyncrasies can make the correct spelling stick in your mind.

Here is the way this type of sounding out would work. Take the word *conscience*. This word is frequently misspelled because it is not pronounced the way it is spelled. To remember how to spell it, you could break the word into its two syllables, *con-science*, pronouncing each as individual words, as they are spelled: *con* and *science*. Similarly, you could exaggerate the pronunciation of *Connecticut* as three words: *connect* and *i* and *cut*. This will help you remember the second *c* in the word.

PRACTICE

Break the following words into syllables and circle the syllable with the primary accent.

1. anger

2. elucidate

3. generous

4. sofa

5. children

6. energy

7. gratitude

8. multiple

9. pillow

10. computer

11. decline

12. surreptitious

13. malignant

14. horticulture

15. banana

16. mire

17. fortitude

18. cabinet

19. clandestine

20. light

ANSWERS

1. an'-ger
2. e-lu'-ci-date
3. gen'-er-ous
4. so'-fa
5. chil'-dren
6. en'-er-gy
7. grat'-i-tude
8. mul'-ti-ple
9. pil'-low
10. com-pu'-ter
11. de-cline'
12. sur-rep-ti'-tious
13. ma-lig'-nant
14. hor'-ti-cul-ture
15. ba-na'-na
16. mire (one syllable)
17. for'-ti-tude
18. cab'-i-net
19. clan-des'-tine
20. light (one syllable)

word meanings

*For a large class of cases—though not for all—in which
we employ the word* meaning *it can be defined thus:
the meaning of a word is its use in the language.*
—LUDWIG WITTGENSTEIN (1889–1951)
AUSTRIAN PHILOSOPHER

THIS MAY SEEM obvious, but when you write a word, you should know what it means. Be aware of what you are trying to say and then make sure that the words you choose convey the right meaning. It is easy to get into the habit of more-or-less knowing what a word means and then using it, whether it is accurate and appropriate or not. This type of lackadaisical word usage can get you into trouble. You may find yourself writing the wrong word in an important essay or letter, not only marring your image in the eyes of the reader but also failing to convey exactly what it is you mean to say.

If you strive to use the right words in all of your writing, however, you will not find yourself in that position. You simply need to think about the words you use and be sure that you know their meanings before using them. When you're not entirely sure of the meaning of a word, but you think it is probably correct in a particular situation, stop and look the word up in your dictionary. Make sure the word is correct. This exercise will help you to learn and to know what words mean, even those that you thought you already knew.

Knowing the meaning of your words is particularly important for homonyms—words that are spelled differently but pronounced alike. It can save you from writing *their* when you really mean *there*, or *compliment* when you want to say *complement*. Thinking about the meaning of the words you are writing will also help you with frequently confused similar words and word forms. For example:

> lose / loose
>
> accept / except
>
> precede / proceed

These word pairs have only subtle sound and spelling differences but they have very different meanings. Do you know the differences? Let's take a look at what each word means, so you can better understand how small differences in spelling can add up to large differences in meaning.

> *Lose* is a verb that means *to come to be without something*, such as through accident or theft, so that there is little or no prospect of recovery. *Lose* is pronounced with a *z* sound instead of an *s* sound.
>
> *Loose* is an adjective that means *the opposite of tight or contained*; *loose* is pronounced with an *s* sound.
>
> *Accept* is a verb that means *to receive, admit, or regard as true*.
>
> *Except* is a preposition that means excluding. It is also a conjunction that means *other than*.
>
> *Precede* is a verb that means *to come before*.
>
> *Proceed* is a verb that means *to go forward*.

As you can see by comparing the meaning of the two words in each set, they have similar spellings but very different meanings.

Being aware of the meaning of words will help you to avoid embarrassing mistakes. Remember, if you don't know what a word means, take the time to look it up in your dictionary. If you can attach meaning to a word, you may find it easier to remember how to spell it. The homonyms covered in Lesson 24 and the confusing words covered in Lesson 26 will be easier to distinguish once you know their meanings.

You might recall spending lots of time in grade school reviewing list after list of vocabulary words in preparation for your weekly spelling test. Although this thought may bring back bad memories, lists can help you learn what words mean. Using the suggestions laid out in Lesson 1, develop a master word list of confusing words, homonyms, and other words that give you trouble, and look up their definitions in the dictionary. Write them out on flash cards and test yourself whenever you have free time, or at a designated time each day or every week. Reviewing the meaning of common word roots, prefixes, and suffixes (covered in Lessons 5, 6, and 7) will add to your knowledge. You will often be able to deduce the meaning of an unfamiliar word by recognizing the root. Spend time learning the word parts and testing yourself with your word list. Soon, you will fully understand what the words on your list mean, and you will never misuse them again.

....

TIP: If you are determined to expand your vocabulary and enhance your knowledge of what various words mean, devote a month to the pursuit. Resolve to look up the definition of at least one word every day. It can be a word on the list of difficult or tricky words that you've created or it can be a word that you heard or read that day. However you come across it, look it up. Read the pronunciation and the definitions. Write out the word and its meaning on a flashcard and then test yourself later. All of these activities will do two things. First, they will make looking words up in your dictionary a habit. Second, they will expand your vocabulary and improve your spelling.

....

PRACTICE

Use your dictionary to look up the definitions of the *italicized* words and then choose the word that best fits the sentence.

1. After Ryan took the pack of gum from the store without paying for it, he was burdened by a guilty *conscience / conscious*.

2. Jorge and Kyle went to Mexico last year and plan to go *their / there* again this winter.

3. Ava walks *passed / past* the grocery store on her way to school.

4. Lucy's shoe was so *loose / lose* it fell off when she walked quickly.

5. Mrs. Crandall planned a party that was sure to *excite / incite* all of the kids.

6. Everyone passed the exam *accept / except* for Gavin.

7. They had to *transmit / submit* the message via fax.

8. Without the key, they couldn't *access / assess* their safety deposit box.

9. We loved to listen to Seamus's Irish *assent / accent*.

10. Abbie took the story seriously, but I thought it was meant as *simile / satire*.

11. The king's *rein / reign* was one of the high points in the country's history.

12. We donated all of the *precedes / proceeds* of the event to charity.

13. If you reach a weight loss plateau, you should *vary / very* your exercise routine.

14. It takes a while to *adapt / adopt* to daylight saving time.

15. Children are considered *minors / miners* until they turn 18.

ANSWERS

1. After Ryan took the pack of gum from the store without paying for it, he was burdened by a guilty *conscience*.
2. Jorge and Kyle went to Mexico last year and plan to go *there* again this winter.
3. Ava walks *past* the grocery store on her way to school.
4. Lucy's shoe was so *loose* it fell off when she walked quickly.
5. Mrs. Crandall planned a party that was sure to *excite* all of the kids.
6. Everyone passed the exam *except* for Gavin.
7. They had to *transmit* the message via fax.
8. Without the key, they couldn't *access* their safety deposit box.
9. We loved to listen to Seamus's Irish *accent*.
10. Abbie took the story seriously, but I thought it was meant as *satire*.
11. The king's *reign* was one of the high points in the country's history.
12. We donated all of the *proceeds* of the event to charity.
13. If you reach a weight loss plateau, you should *vary* your exercise routine.
14. It takes a while to *adapt* to daylight saving time.
15. Children are considered *minors* until they turn 18.

S E C T I O N 2

word parts and forms

AT THEIR MOST basic, words are made up of letters: vowels and consonants that combine in a specific order to create a word. The way words are formed is far from random, however. Words have roots to which prefixes and suffixes are added to form the words that we use in daily life. These roots are common among many different words; learning the meaning of the roots, along with the meaning of the many prefixes and suffixes, can help you to more easily remember how to spell.

Once words are formed, they are categorized by the part of speech they represent. Words can be nouns, pronouns, verbs, adjectives, adverbs, prepositions, conjunctions, or interjections. The lessons in this section will help you to understand word parts—the roots, prefixes, and suffixes—as well as letter combinations and verb conjugations.

roots

*Give me a word, any word, and I show
you that the root of that word is Greek.*
—GUS PORTOKALOS, CHARACTER IN
MY BIG FAT GREEK WEDDING

A key to better spelling is to understand the meaning of words. A key to understanding the meaning of words is to understand the meanings of their parts. In this lesson, we'll explain the most basic part of words, the root.

A ROOT WORD is the most basic form of a word. It is the base from which another word is made and it is the part of a word that holds the most meaning. Every word either *is* a root or *has* a root. Roots combine with prefixes and suffixes (which are covered in Lessons 6 and 7) to make words.

Most roots come from ancient Greek and Latin words (such as *dem*, meaning *people*, for example), and many have become quite common in the English language. Let's look at an example. The root *cycl*, which means *circle* or *wheel* is used to form the words *bicycle*, *motorcycle*, and *tricycle* by adding the prefixes *bi* (two), *motor* (motor), and *tri* (three). Knowing what the root means will enable you to understand the meaning of a word and spell it more accurately and confidently. In the case of our examples, by looking at the root and the prefixes, you can see that *bicycle* can be broken down into its parts to mean *two wheels*. Similarly, *tricycle* means *three wheels* and *motorcycle* means *motorized* wheels.

It is important to understand roots and become familiar with them in order to fully understand how to spell well. Learning some of the most common roots will provide you with a foundation on which to build that knowledge.

....

TIP: Although some roots are words unto themselves—for example, *finite* and *vast* are both words and roots—most roots cannot stand on their own as words. Let's look, for example, at the root *cred*, which means *believe*. You wouldn't say that you *cred in ghosts*, even if you do, because *cred* doesn't stand on its own. When you add a prefix or suffix, such as *in-* and *-ible* to make *incredible*, then you have words. Now you can take the root, *cred*, and use it in your speech. "Seeing that ghost was *incredible*!"

....

COMMON WORD ROOTS

The following table lists many of the most common word roots, along with their meanings and examples of words with those roots. This list is provided to help you become familiar with the common roots. Don't be intimidated by the list! Yes, it is a long list. But you don't need to learn every root listed here. You simply need to start to recognize the most common roots and then you can begin to build upon that knowledge.

One way to tackle word roots is to pick 10 to 20 roots to review each week. Create flash cards based on the roots you've chosen and test yourself throughout the week, whenever you have free time. You'll be amazed at how quickly word roots start to make sense and become familiar to you.

Root	Meaning	Example
aco(u)	hear, hearing	acoustic
act, ag	act, do, drive	active, agent
agon, agonist	struggle, contend	agony, antagonist
alter	other	alternate, alter ego
ambul	walk	amble, circumambulate
ami, amic	love	amiable, amicable
amphi	all sides	amphibian
andro, andry	male	androgynous, polyandry

Root	Meaning	Example
ann, enni	year	anniversary, perennial
aqua, aque	water	aquatic, aqueduct
arch	first, chief, leader	archangel, archaic
aud	to hear, sound	audible, audience
auto	by oneself	autobiography, autodidact
bell	war	antebellum, belligerent
bene, bon	good	benefit, bonus
biblio	book	bibliography, bibliophile
bio	life	biography, biology
brev	short	abbreviate, brevity
cap, cep	take, seize	accept, capture
capit, capt	head, chief	capital, captain
caus, cuse	cause	causal, excuse
ced, ceed	yield, go	recede, proceed
chrom	color	chromatic, monochrome
chron	time	chronicle, synchronize
cis, cise	cut	excise, incision, scissors
cogn	know, think	recognize, incognito
corp	body	corpse, corporal
cosm	universe, order	cosmic, cosmopolitan
cred	believe	credible, credit, credo
crypt	hidden	cryptogram, cryptic
culp	guilt	culpable, culprit
dem	people	democracy, epidemic
dent	tooth	dentist, dentifrice
derm	skin	dermatology, epidermis
dic, dict	say, speak	dictate, edict, indicate,
dom	house, master	domestic, dominate
dox	belief, opinion	orthodox, paradox
duc, duct	lead	conduct, deduce, seduction
ego	self	egotist, egomania
equ	equal	equity, equate, equidistant

Root	Meaning	Example
fac	make, do	benefactor, factory
fid, fidel	faith, trust	confidence, fidelity
fin, finite	end, purpose	definite, infinite
flu, flux	to flow	affluence, fluid, influx
for, fort	strong	enforce, fortress
frater	brother	fraternal, fraternity
gen, gon	birth, race	congenital, gender, gonad
ger, gest	carry, produce	digest, gestate, gesture
grad, grade, gress	step	biodegrade, gradual, progress
gram, graph	write	autograph, telegram
greg	society, group	aggregate, gregarious
hema, hemo	blood	hematology, hemoglobin
hol, holo	whole	holistic, hologram
hydr, hydro	water	dehydrate, hydrant
idi, idio	personal	idiom, idiosyncratic
iso	equal	isometric, isotope
ject	throw	eject, inject, reject
jud, jur, just	judge, law	adjudicate, judge, justice
jug, junct	a link, to join	conjunction, conjugate
lat, late, lation	bear, carry	collate, correlate, legislation
lev, lieve	to lift, light in weight	alleviate, elevator, relieve
lign, line	line	align, delineate, lineage
liter	letter	literature, illiterate, literal
loc	place	local, location
locut, loqu, loquy	to speak, speech	locution, colloquy
log, logue, logy, lexico	speech, word, study of	logic, lexicon, analogy
luc, lumin	light, to shine	illuminate, lucent, luminary
macro	large	macrocosm
magn	large	magnify, magnificent
mal	bad	malady, malcontent
man	hand	manufacture, manuscript

Root	Meaning	Example
mar	sea	marine, mariner
mater	mother	maternal, maternity
medi, meso, mid	in the middle of	amidst, mediocre, mesoderm
micro	small	microscope, microcosm
min	small	minority, minuscule, minute
mis	hate	misanthrope, misogyny
mit, miss	send	permit, submission, mission
mob, mot, mov	move	immovable, mobile, promote
mon	warn	premonition, admonition
mor, mort	death	moribund, mortician, mortify
morph	form, structure	metamorphosis, amorphous
mut	change	mutant, mutability, mutate
neg	to deny	negate, neglect, renege
neo	new	neologism, neonate
neuro	nerve	neurology, neurosis
noct, nox	night	nocturnal, equinox
opt, optic	eye, vision	optics, option
pac	peace	pacify, pacifist
par, pare	equal	parity, compare
pater	father	paternal, paternity, patricide
path, pathic, pathy	emotion, suffering	pathetic, empathic, sympathy
ped, pod	foot	pedal, pedometer, podiatrist
pend	hang, weigh	pendulum, pendant, suspend
phil, philia	love, fondness for	philosophy, philanthropy
plan	flat	planar, plantation, plane
plaud, plaus, plod, plos	make a loud noise	applaud, explode, plosive
plen, plet	to fill, full	plentiful, plethora, replenish
port	carry	portable, transport, report
pot	power	potent, omnipotent, potentate
prim, prin	first	primary, primate, principal
quest, quir, quisit	to ask	question, acquire, inquisition

Root	Meaning	Example
qui, quit	rest	quiet, quit, acquiesce, acquit
rect, reg	to rule or guide; proper	rectify, regal, region
rupt	break, sever	abrupt, disrupt, interrupt
salu, salv	safety, health	salubrious, salvage, salutary
scent, scend	climb	ascend, ascent
schizo, schiz	division, split	schizophrenic
sci	know	scientific
sciss	cut	scissors
scrib, script	write	manuscript, proscribe
sec, sect	cut	dissect, section
secut, sequ	follow, ensue	sequence, consequence
sed, sess	sit	sedentary, session
sen, senil	old, old age	senior, senator, senility
sens, sent	feel, be aware	sensible, sentient
sequ, secu	follow	sequence, sequel, consecutive
simil	same	similar, assimilate, simile
solute, solv	release, loosen, free	dissolve, absolute, insoluble
son	sound	sonar, resonate, unison
soph	wisdom, knowledge	philosophy, sophisticate
spec, spect, spic	look, see	aspect, specific, suspicious
spir, spire	to breathe, breath, spirit	aspire, expire, conspire
stant, stat, stent	to stand, to stay, position	assistant, consistent, station
stru, struct	build	destructive, instruct, obstruct
tact, tang	touch	tactile, tangible,
temper, tempor, temp	time, balance	temporize, temporary
ten, tent	hold	tentative, tenable, tenuous
terr	earth	subterranean, terrain
theo	god, deity	theology, polytheism, atheist
top	place	topic, topology, utopia

Root	Meaning	Example
rib, tribe, trit	rub, wear down	tribulation, trite, attrition
trop, tropic, tropy	to turn; a change or turn	entropy, trope, tropical
uro	urine	urologist
vac, van, vast	empty, desolate	devastate, vacuum, vanity
val	to be strong, to be worthy	valiant, valor, validate
ven, vent	come, go	intervention, convene
ver, veri	truth	veracious, verdict, verify
ver, vert	turn	introvert, irreversible, vertigo
vit, viv	life, to live	vital, survive, vivify
voc, vow	voice, to call or summon	avow, vocalize, vociferous
vol	will, desire, wish	volition, volunteer
vor, vorous, vour	eat, swallow	voracious, carnivorous, devour
xeno	foreign	xenophobe, xenogamy
zoa, zo, zoo, zoon	life, living	zoo, zodiac, metazoan, protozoon

PRACTICE

Match the root with the correct meaning.

Root	Meaning
1. lat	**a.** to bear, to carry
2. trop	**b.** large
3. path	**c.** hold
4. macro	**d.** lead

5. duc   e. empty, desolate

6. vac   f. to turn, a change or turn

7. ann   g. sit

8. ten   h. hand

9. sed   i. year

10. man   j. emotion, suffering

Identify the root in the following words:

11. epidermis

12. rectify

13. consecutive

14. plantation

15. synchronize

16. amicable

17. lucent

18. dominate

19. fluid

20. antebellum

ANSWERS

1. **a.** to bear, to carry
2. **f.** to turn, a change or turn
3. **j.** emotion, suffering
4. **b.** large
5. **d.** lead
6. **e.** empty, desolate
7. **i.** year
8. **h.** hold
9. **g.** sit
10. **h.** hand
11. derm
12. rect
13. sec
14. plan
15. chron
16. ami
17. luc
18. dom
19. flu
20. bell

prefixes

The beginning is the most important part of the work.
—PLATO (428/427–348/347 B.C.)
GREEK PHILOSOPHER AND FOUNDER OF THE ACADEMY IN ATHENS

Prefixes are another important word part. They combine with roots and suffixes to form words. This lesson will explain what they are and how to understand their meanings.

IN LESSON 5, we looked at roots and how they are the building blocks of words. A prefix is another word part; it is added in front of the root to create a word. Suffixes, which we'll cover in Lesson 7, are added *after* the root. Like roots, prefixes have fixed meanings that remain the same no matter to which word they are attached. By adding a prefix to a word or root, you will enhance or change its meaning.

Although you cannot tell the meaning of a word from the prefix alone, the prefix can help you get an idea of what the word is about. In fact, you can look at the prefix of *prefix* to determine the meaning: *pre-* means *before* and the root, *fix*, means *fix* or *attach*. So, by combining the meanings, you can figure out that *prefix* means *attach before*. And that is exactly what you do with a prefix: You attach it before the root. In other words, a prefix appears at the beginning of a word.

Let's look at another one. The prefix *omni-*, for example, means *all*. This prefix can be found in the words *omnipresent*, which means *all present*, and *omnivore*, which means *someone that eats all foods*. Now, let's apply your knowledge of this prefix to another word. Read the following sentence:

When Tyler became the team captain, he started to act as if he was *omnipotent*.

What does *omnipotent* mean? You know that the prefix means *all* so you already know that the word means all *something*. Going back to what you learned in Lesson 5, can you find the root? Since the root is *pot*, which means *powerful*, you can correctly deduce that *omnipotent* means *all powerful*. This exercise is one that you can repeat with any new word you encounter. Break the word into its parts, determine the meanings of those parts, and then string the individual meanings together to get to the full meaning of the word. If you're still unsure, take a peek into your dictionary, or refer to the lists in this book.

....

TIP: Many prefixes have similar or the same meanings, such as *dis-*, *il-*, and *un-*. They are not always interchangeable, however, because their subtle differences will either change the meaning of a word or simply make it wrong. The former is the case with *disable* and *unable*. While their meanings are similar, there is a distinct difference. *Disable* is a verb that means to deprive of capability or effectiveness, especially to impair the physical abilities of, and to make incapable of performing a certain action. *Unable*, on the other hand, is an adjective that means lacking the necessary power, authority, or means; not able, incapable, and lacking the mental or physical capability or efficiency; and incompetent.

As you grow familiar with the meanings and nuances of prefixes, you will become better equipped to choose the correct one to use in any situation.

....

COMMON PREFIXES

This list of prefixes covers the most common prefixes, their meanings, and some examples of words using each prefix. Review this list just as you did the list of roots in Lesson 5.

Prefix	Meaning	Example
a-	not, without	atypical, amorphous
ab-	from, away	abnormal, abscond
ante-	before	antecedent, antemeridian
anti-	against	antipathy, antihistamine
bi-	two	binoculars, bicycle
circum-	around	circumference, circumspect
co-, con-	with, together	to coexist, conference, to contribute
counter-	opposite	counterpart, counterclockwise
contr-	against	contraband, controversy
de-	down, away from	to debark, deplete
dec-	ten	decimal, to decimate
dis-	not, opposite of	disengaged, disloyal
eu-	good, well	euphoric, euphemism
ex-	out of, away from	extract, exhume
hyper-	above	hyperbole, hyperactive
hypo-	below	hypocrite, hypodermic
il-	not, opposite	illogic, illegal
in-	in, within	induct, inculcate
inter-	between	intermittent, interplay
intra-	within	intranet, intramural
intro-	into, within	introvert, introduction
mis-	bad, wrong	misspell, misanthrope
neo-	new, recent	neonatal, neophyte
non-	not	nonchalant, nonconformist
over-	exceeding	overabundance, override
poly-	many, much	polytechnic, polygamy
post-	after	postmortem, postwar
pre-	before	preview, prepare
pro-	before	proceed, progress
re-	again	review, repent
retro-	back, again	retrograde, retroactive
semi-	half, partly	semiannual, semiconductor

Prefix	Meaning	Example
sub-	under	substrate, sublimate
super-	above, over	superficial, superscript
syn-	with, together	synthesis, synonym
trans-	across	transmit, transfer
tri-	three	triad, triangle
un-	not	unable, unacceptable

NUMERICAL PREFIXES

Several prefixes refer to numbers; thinking about them as a group may help you to remember them better. Here is a list of numerical prefixes that you will routinely come across.

Prefix	Meaning	Example
mono-	one	monotype, monologue
uni-	one	universal, unilateral
bi-	two	biweekly, biannual
di-	two	divide, diverge
tri-	three	trinity, trilogy
quad-	four	quadrangle
quart-	fourth	quarter
penta-	five	pentagon, pentameter
quint-	five	quintet, quintuplets
hex-	six	hexagon, hexameter
sex-	six	sextuplets, sextillion
sept-	seven	septet, septennial
oct-	eight	octopus, octave
non-	nine	nonagon, nonagenarian
dec-	ten	decimal, decade
cent-	hundred	century, centipede
mill-	thousand	millennium
kilo-	thousand	kilobyte
mega-	million	megabyte, megaton

PRACTICE

In each of the following sentences, choose the word that uses the correct prefix.

1. Andrew was *unheartened* / *disheartened* to learn that he was rejected from his first-choice college.

2. They were reading about the *antebellum* / *antibellum* period in the South, the time before the start of the Civil War.

3. The meteorologist called for *intermittent* / *intramittent* rain showers.

4. Ever since Mrs. Smith gave birth to her *quintuplets* / *sextuplets*, people have been giving her five sets of every gift!

5. They were able to see the play during the *review* / *preview* period, two weeks before it opened.

6. Casey and Carolyn wanted to play on the same *intermural* / *intramural* team, but their gym teacher separated them.

7. Brady wished he could make more friends, but he was just a natural *introvert* / *intervert*.

8. He felt constant pain in his arm after *hypoextending* / *hyperextending* his elbow.

9. The *pretest* / *protest* was difficult for all the students in the class because they hadn't yet learned algebra.

10. She needed to find another word with the same meaning as *important*, so she opened her thesaurus and looked for *synonyms* / *antonyms*.

ANSWERS

1. Andrew was *disheartened* to learn that he was rejected from his first-choice college.
2. They were reading about the *antebellum* period in the South, the time before the start of the Civil War.
3. The meteorologist called for *intermittent* rain showers.
4. Ever since Mrs. Smith gave birth to her *quintuplets*, people have been giving her five sets of every gift!
5. They were able to see the play during the *preview* period, two weeks before it opened.
6. Casey and Carolyn wanted to play on the same *intramural* team, but their gym teacher separated them.
7. Brady wished he could make more friends, but he was just a natural *introvert*.
8. He felt constant pain in his arm after *hyperextending* his elbow.
9. The *pretest* was difficult for all the students in the class because they hadn't yet learned algebra.
10. She needed to find another word with the same meaning as *important*, so she opened her thesaurus and looked for *synonyms*.

suffixes

Learning isn't a means to an end; it is an end in itself.
—ROBERT A. HEINLEIN (1907–1988)
AMERICAN NOVELIST AND SCIENCE FICTION WRITER

Like prefixes, suffixes are added to roots to create new words. In this lesson, you will learn the origins of suffixes and how to understand and identify them.

A SUFFIX IS similar to a prefix, except that it is added to the end of a word to form a new one, instead of the beginning. There are other differences as well. For example, unlike prefixes, more than one suffix can be added to a word. If you look at the word *beautifully*, for instance, you can see that two suffixes, *-ful* and *-ly*, have been added to *beauty* to create the new word.

Technically, suffixes include plural endings and conjugation endings. However, in this book, we've covered both of those topics elsewhere (see Lessons 20 and 21 for plurals and Lessons 9 and 10 for conjugations) so this lesson will focus on suffix endings that change a word from one part of speech to another. A part of speech is how a word is used rather than what a word is: for example, a word might be used as a noun in one sentence but as a verb in another.

TIP: Not all parts of speech can take all endings. This chart will show which endings can be added to the different parts of speech.

Part of Speech	Job	Examples	Common Endings
noun	names a person, place, thing, or idea	roads, theses, carpenter, wilderness, advantage, miscreant, element	*-s, -es, -er, -ness, -age, -ant, -ent*
verb	names an action	plays, goes, waiting, wanted, identify, embolden	*-s, -es, -ing, -ed, -ify, -en*
adjective	modifies a noun or a pronoun	tolerable, contemptible, beautiful, frantic, clueless, pretty	*-able, -ible, -ful, -ic, -less, -y*
adverb	modifies a verb, an adjective, another adverb, a clause, or a sentence	quietly	*-ly*

Some words change when certain suffixes are added to them. For instance, many words ending in a silent *e* will drop the *-e* before adding *-ed* and *-ing*, as in the word *love*. *Love* becomes *loved* and *loving*. See Lesson 23 for more on keeping and dropping a final *e*. Words ending in a *consonant* and *-y* change the *-y* to an *-i* before adding *-ed*. Many of those words, however, do not make any change when adding *-ing*. For example, *supply* becomes *supplied* and *supplying*. Words that end in a *vowel* and *-y*, on the other hand, add both *-ed* and *-ing* without making any changes. The word *delay*, for example, becomes *delayed* and *delaying*. For more on when and how to change a final *y*, see Lesson 22.

Don't let the required changes confuse you. The rules for adding suffixes are actually fairly straightforward and consistent. There are six main rules that you will need to learn to ensure that you use suffixes properly. Let's look at them one at a time.

1. If a suffix begins with consonant, it usually can be added to a word that ends in a consonant or a silent *e* with no change to the word or the suffix. Some examples include *good + ness = goodness, quick + ly = quickly, love + ly = lovely*. Some notable exceptions to this rule include *argument, awful, duly, judgment, ninth, truly, wholly,* and *wisdom*. Since there are far fewer exceptions than words that follow the rule, take a little time to commit them to memory.

2. If a word ends in a silent *e* and the suffix begins with a vowel, drop the *-e* before adding the ending. For example, *move + able = movable* and *fortune + ate = fortunate*.

3. If a word ends with a consonant followed by a *y*, change the *-y* to an *-i* before adding the ending. If the word ends in a vowel plus *-y*, keep the final *y*. For example, *happy + ness = happiness* and *marry + age = marriage*. On the other hand, *pay + ment = payment* and *destroy + er = destroyer*.

4. If a one-syllable word ends in a consonant-plus-vowel combination, double the final consonant when adding a suffix that begins with a vowel. Examples of doubling the final consonant include *tip + ing = tipping, rot + en = rotten,* and *set + ing = setting*. Remember that this rule applies only to suffixes that begin with vowels. You do not need to double the final consonants when adding a suffix that begins with a consonant, like *fear + less = fearless*. Also, this rule does not apply to words with *-w* or *-x* as their final consonant, for example *follow + er = follower, flex + ing = flexing*.

5. If a polysyllabic word ends in a consonant-plus-vowel-plus-consonant combination and the accent is on the final syllable, double the final consonant when adding a suffix that begins with a vowel. Phew! That's a long rule. It is less confusing than it appears, though. Examples of words that take this rule include *excel* (accent is on the second syllable) *+ ent = excellent, begin* (accent is on the second syllable) *+ ing = beginning,* and *submit* (accent is on the second syllable) + ing = submitting.

6. If a word ends in any other combination of vowels and consonants, do not double the final consonant when adding an ending. This rule means that these other combinations take suffixes without requiring any change to the word or the suffix. Some examples are *beat + ing = beating*, *comfort + able = comfortable*, and *read + ing = reading*.

COMMON SUFFIXES

This list covers the most common suffixes, their meanings, and some examples of words using each prefix. The suffixes are categorized by their type: whether they are noun, adjective, or verb endings.

Review this list just as you did the list of roots in Lesson 5 and the list of prefixes in Lesson 6.

NOUN ENDINGS

Suffix	Meaning	Example
-age	action or process; house; rank	drainage, orphanage, marriage
-al	action or process	rehearsal, disposal, reversal
-an, -ian	of or related to; a person specializing in	guardian, historian
-ance, -ence	action or process, state of	adolescence, dalliance
-ancy, -ency	quality or state	agency, vacancy, latency
-ant, -ent	one that causes action, state	dissident, miscreant, student
-ary	thing belonging to, connected with	adversary, dignitary, library
-cide	killer, killing	suicide, homicide, pesticide
-cy	action or practice, state, quality of	democracy, legitimacy, supremacy
-er, -or	one that is, does, or performs	builder, foreigner, sensor, voter
-ion, -tion	act or process, state, or condition	demolition, dominion, persecution
-ism	act, practice, or process; doctrine	criticism, feminism, imperialism
-ist	one who does	cellist, anarchist, feminist
-ity	quality, state, degree	calamity, amity, veracity

-ment	action or process, result, object	entertainment, amusement
-ness	state, condition, quality, degree	happiness, kindness, quickness
-ology	doctrine, science, theory	biology, theology
-or	condition, activity	candor, succor, valor
-sis	process or action	diagnosis, metamorphosis
-ure	act or process, office, or function	censure, legislature, exposure
-y	state or condition, activity	laundry, sympathy, anarchy

ADJECTIVE ENDINGS

Suffix	Meaning	Example
-able, -ible	capable or worthy of, tending to	flammable, discernible, culpable
-al, -ial, -ical	having the quality of, relating to	educational, historical, social
-an, -ian	one who is or does; related to	human, agrarian, simian
-ant, -ent	performing or being	important, incessant, independent
-ful	full of, tending or liable to	peaceful, wishful, hopeful
-ic	pertaining or relating to	chronic, scenic, fantastic
-ile	tending to, capable of	futile, senile, fragile
-ish	having the quality of	Spanish, bookish, selfish
-ive	performing or tending toward	cooperative, supportive, sensitive
-less	without, lacking, unable to act	endless, fearless, sleepless
-ous, -ose	full of, relating to	adventurous, generous, bellicose
-y	characterized by, tending to	sleepy, hungry, cursory

VERB ENDINGS

Suffix	Meaning	Example
-ate	to make, to cause to be	violate, emanate, detonate, tolerate
-en	cause to be or have; come to be	quicken, strengthen, frighten
-ify, -fy	to make, form into	beautify, sanctify, rectify
-ize	cause to be or become, bring about	synchronize, colonize, realize

PRACTICE

Select the correctly spelled word from each set of three. Use your dictionary to learn any of the words that you do not know.

1. drawing   drawwing   draing

2. respectible   respectable   respectabel

3. comfortting   comforrting   comforting

4. pitiful   pityful   pittiful

5. referral   referal   referel

6. paiment   payment   payyment

7. employable   emploiable   emploable

8. arguement   argument   argumment

9. peted   petted   peteed

10. happily   happyly   hapily

11. transmiting   transmitting   transsmiting

12. annoyance   annoiance   anoyance

13. walkking   walking   wallking

14. breezey   breezzy   breezy

15. teacher   teachher   teacheer

ANSWERS

1. drawing
2. respectable
3. comforting
4. pitiful
5. referral
6. payment
7. employable
8. argument
9. petted
10. happily
11. transmitting
12. annoyance
13. walking
14. breezy
15. teacher

compound words

English is a funny language; that explains why we park our car on the driveway and drive our car on the parkway.

—Anonymous

Putting two words together is often as simple as adding one word to the other. Sometimes, though, combining words requires a hyphen or it requires the words to remain separate, even though they become one idea. This lesson will explain how to create compound words.

SOMETIMES IT MAY seem that we can join any two words by simply adding one to the other. After all, new buzzwords appear every day that combine two separate words to create new meaning—for instance, *website*. It is certainly true that new words can be created by adding one to the other; there are thousands of compound words in the English language. Some compound words, however, are more readily accepted than others. There are rules about when a compound word should be written as one word, as a hyphenated word, or as separate words with one meaning. Conversely, there are some words that should be written as compound words but that are often mistakenly written as two separate words.

You might think there is little or no difference between words written as two separate words or as a single, compound word, but in fact the difference in meaning can be significant. A *soft ball*, for example, is any ball that is soft. But the word *softball* has a more specialized meaning: it is the ball used in the game of softball.

First, let's take a closer look at compound words. There are technically three forms of compound words. The first form—what you probably think of when you hear the term *compound word*—is the closed form. In the closed form, two words are joined together to create one word. For example, *childlike, redhead, laptop, paperback,* and *mailroom* are all closed-form compound words.

The second form is the hyphenated form, which may consist of more than two words. This form includes words like *self-conscious, sister-in-law,* and *over-the-counter* (when used as an adjective). Hyphenated words are covered in Lesson 17. You might want to look ahead to that lesson while reviewing this one, in order to learn about hyphens.

The third form of compound words is the open form. Words such as *real estate, post office, blue collar,* and *middle class* are in this category. This is the category that people most often fail to think of as compound words. However, the two words work together as one unit.

To further confuse matters, some words are accepted when written in any of the three forms, while some absolutely are not. Moreover (which is a compound word!), some words begin as open-form compounds and, over time, become written as hyphenated compound words and, finally, as closed-form compound words. Generally speaking, compound words morph in their forms because of accepted usage. As a word begins to be written more and more as a hyphenated word, for example, instead of as two separate words, the hyphenated form will become the more accepted and standard form.

TIP: Since compound words have been known to change over time, the best way to be sure you are spelling a word correctly is to look it up in a good, up-to-date dictionary. You can also rely on style and usage guides to explain the most current forms for compound words. If you are writing an essay for a class, you might want to ask your teacher to tell you the accepted form for the word in question. For example, some usage guides write *Web site*, while others write *web-site* and still others write *website*. Which one is correct? It depends on where it is being written and the style guidelines that govern it. The bottom line is that when you are unsure of how the recipient of your work would like a word written, you should ask!

When creating closed-form compound words, there is a simple rule to keep in mind. Two individual words in succession can be combined into one compound word if the combination creates one idea or item. That is the key for compound words. If the two words do not create one idea or item, then they should always stay separate. In most cases, when creating the closed-form compound word, you will keep the spelling of the individual words intact, as with a word like *ladybug*.

But what about hyphens? In certain specific instances, hyphens are used to create compound words. A compound adjective that appears *before* the noun is hyphenated: for example, *light-blue umbrella*. Other situations in which hyphens are used to join words are covered in Lesson 17.

COMMONLY CONFUSED COMPOUND WORDS

As with most word types in the English language, there are some that are particularly tricky and confusing. Words like *alright* and *all right* are often confused. The same is true of *maybe* and *may be*, and *anyway*, and *any way*. Such words cause confusion because they have slightly different meanings when written as one closed-form compound word versus two distinct, individual words. You will find more information on confusing words in Lesson 27.

LIST OF CLOSED-FORM COMPOUND WORDS

Here is a list of closed-form compound words. It is by no means a complete list, but it will give you an idea of the range of words that are considered compound words. You may wish to read through the list and note any words that you do not know, and look them up in your dictionary.

afterlife	another	anywhere
afternoon	anybody	around
airfield	anyhow	babysitter
airplane	anymore	backache
airport	anyone	backbone
airtime	anyplace	backbreaker
allover	anytime	backdrop
alongside	anyway	backfire

background	bookkeeper	crossover
backhand	bookmark	crosswalk
backlog	bookmobile	daybook
backpack	bookshelf	daybreak
backside	bookstore	daydream
backslap	bookworm	daylight
backspace	bowtie	daytime
backspin	brainchild	deadline
backstage	butterball	dishwasher
backtrack	butterflies	dishwater
backward	buttermilk	dogwood
backyard	bypass	doorstep
ballroom	cannot	doorstop
baseball	cardboard	downbeat
basketball	cardstock	drawbridge
because	carefree	driveway
become	caretaker	earthquake
bedroom	carfare	eggshell
bellbottom	cargo	elsewhere
blackball	carhop	everything
blackberries	carload	eyeballs
blackbird	carpetbagger	eyesight
blackboard	carpool	fireball
blackjack	carport	firebomb
blacklist	carryall	firecracker
blackmail	carsick	firefighter
blackout	cartwheel	fireflies
blacksmith	catwalk	firehouse
blacktop	caveman	fireproof
bluefish	clockwise	fireworks
bodywork	coffeemaker	fisherman
boldface	commonplace	fishpond
bookcase	cornmeal	fishtail
bookend	courtyard	football

footnote	grandstand	keynote
footprints	grasshopper	keypad
forbear	graveyard	keystroke
forbid	gumball	keyway
forearm	hamburger	keyword
forefather	handcuff	lifeblood
forefinger	headquarters	lifeboat
foregone	herein	lifeguard
foreground	herself	lifelike
forehand	highway	lifeline
forehead	himself	lifelong
foreleg	homebound	lifesaver
foreman	homemade	lifetime
foresee	hometown	lifework
foreshadow	honeybee	limelight
forethought	honeycomb	limestone
foretold	honeydew	lukewarm
forewarn	honeymoon	mainland
forget	honeysuckle	matchbox
forgive	hookup	meantime
forklift	horseback	meanwhile
format	household	moonbeam
fortnight	housekeeper	moonlight
glassmaking	houseplant	moonlit
goodnight	however	moonwalk
grandchild	inside	moreover
grandchildren	intake	motorcycle
granddaughter	itself	nearby
grandfather	jailbait	newborn
grandmaster	jellybean	newscaster
grandmother	jellyfish	newsletter
grandnieces	jetliner	newsman
grandparent	keyboard	newspaper
grandson	keyhole	newsprint

newsreel	repairman	sunbathe
newsstand	riverbank	sundown
newsworthy	sandstone	sunflower
nightfall	saucepan	sunglasses
nobody	scapegoat	sunroof
noisemaker	scarecrow	supercharge
northeast	schoolhouse	superego
notebook	schoolwork	superfine
notepad	seashore	superhero
nowhere	setback	superhuman
oneself	shortbread	superman
overabundance	sidekick	supermarket
overboard	sidewalk	supernatural
overcoat	silversmith	superpower
overflow	skateboard	superscript
overland	snowdrift	supersensitive
pacemaker	softball	supersonic
pancake	somebody	superstar
passbook	someday	superstructure
passkey	somehow	supertanker
passport	someone	superwoman
paycheck	someplace	tabletop
peacemaker	something	tadpole
peppermint	sometimes	tailbone
pickup	somewhat	takeover
pinstripe	somewhere	taxicab
plaything	southwest	taxpayer
popcorn	spearmint	teacup
racquetball	spokesperson	teamwork
railroad	standby	teapot
rainbow	stopwatch	teenager
rainwater	storeroom	textbook
rattlesnake	subway	therefore

throwaway	upgrade	upwind
throwback	upheaval	washcloth
thunderbird	upheld	washout
thunderstorm	uphill	washroom
timesaving	uphold	washstand
timeshare	upkeep	wastepaper
today	upland	watchdog
together	uplift	watchmaker
toolbox	uplink	watchtower
toothpaste	upload	watercolor
toothpick	upon	waterfall
touchdown	uppercase	waterfront
township	upperclassman	waterline
turnkey	uppercut	watermark
turnoff	uppermost	watermelon
underachieve	upright	waterproof
underage	uprising	waterscape
underbelly	uproar	watershed
underbid	uproot	waterside
undercharge	upscale	waterspout
underclothes	upshot	watertight
undercover	upside	waterway
undercurrent	upstage	weatherman
undercut	upstairs	weekend
underdog	upstanding	whatever
underestimate	upstart	wheelbarrow
underexpose	upstate	whitecap
underfoot	upstream	whitefish
underground	uptake	whitewall
upbeat	uptight	whitewash
upbringing	uptown	widespread
upcoming	upturn	without
update	upward	woodshop
upend		

TIP: Pay attention to the material in Lessons 6 and 7 on prefixes and suffixes. The rules outlined in those chapters will give you a better understanding of how to form compound words.

PRACTICE

Select the correct word or words to complete each sentence.

1. Maddie led the *sightseers / sight seers* on a mountain hike.

2. I like to keep my *household / house hold* tidy and organized.

3. When I saw Tom's new *lap top / laptop* I thought, "Wow! What a *supercomputer / super computer*!"

4. The police targeted a radius of four blocks for a crime *crackdown / crack down*.

5. No one likes to ride with Olivia because she drives like she has a *lead foot / leadfoot*.

6. The southern exposure and large windows make this a very *hothouse / hot house*.

7. Do you know the secret *catchphrase / catch phrase*?

8. The plane will not leave until we are all *onboard / on board*.

9. I'd like to find a way to avoid being *bed ridden / bedridden* because of my terrible *back ache / backache*.

10. If Julia's *roommate / room mate* decides to move out, I plan to move in.

ANSWERS

1. Maddie led the *sightseers* on a mountain hike.
2. I like to keep my *household* tidy and organized.
3. When I saw Tom's new *laptop* I thought, "Wow! What a *super computer*!"
4. The police targeted a radius of four blocks for a crime *crackdown*.
5. No one likes to ride with Olivia because she drives like she has a *lead foot*.
6. The southern exposure and large windows make this a very *hot house*.
7. Do you know the secret *catchphrase*?
8. The plane will not leave until we are all *on board*.
9. I'd like to find a way to avoid being *bedridden* because of my terrible *backache*.
10. If Julia's *roommate* decides to move out, I plan to move in.

regular verbs

Life is a verb.
—CHARLOTTE PERKINS GILMAN (1860–1935)
AMERICAN SOCIOLOGIST AND AUTHOR

This lesson will explain the various verb tenses and show you how to conjugate verbs properly.

VERBS ARE EXTREMELY important in the English language. Defined as *the part of speech that expresses existence, action, or occurrence*, verbs allow us to communicate clearly about the past, the present, and the future. If our language didn't have verbs, we wouldn't be able to say where we have been, what we are doing, what we are thinking, or where we will be going. We could point to objects and say their names, but we wouldn't be able to express any action.

The rules for conjugating verbs can be confusing. Most of the confusion, however, surrounds what we call irregular verbs, which are covered in Lesson 10. For regular verbs, the rules are more straightforward. Once you begin to understand the various tenses and forms, you will see some spelling patterns emerge that will reduce your confusion.

Every verb in the English language has three basic tenses that help us to understand when something is going to happen or has happened: in the present, the past, or the future. The tenses can be subdivided into three categories: simple, progressive, and perfect. The following chart gives an example of the categories and tenses of the verb *to hike*.

	Simple	**Progressive**	**Perfect**
Present	hike	am/is/are hiking	have/has hiked
Past	hiked	was/were hiking	had hiked
Future	will hike	will be hiking	will have hiked

We'll work through each of the tenses to describe how verbs are conjugated.

SIMPLE

The simple category is comprised of the present tense, the past tense, and the future tense.

Present Tense

The present tense indicates present action (action that is happening now) or action that happens on a regular basis.

> I *walk* four miles three times a week.

This tense is fairly easy. The basic form of a verb is known as the infinitive form. *To bathe* and *to imagine* are two examples of the infinitive form. The present-tense form is the infinitive of the verb, minus the word *to*. So, *bathe* is the present-tense form of *to bathe* and *imagine* is the present-tense form of *to imagine*.

Past Tense

The past tense indicates action that has already happened (action that occurred in the past).

> Henry *called* when he arrived at Connor's house.

The past tense is formed by taking the infinitive form of the verb, minus the word *to*, and adding *-d* or *-ed*. For example, *grill* becomes *grilled* and *sway* becomes *swayed*. Some verbs change forms when taking the past tense. *Imply*, for example, drops the final *y* and adds *-ied* to make *implied*, and for *repel* the final consonant is doubled before adding *-ed* to make *repelled*. Endings are covered in greater detail in Lessons 7, 22, 23, and 24.

TIP: Here are some tips to keep in mind when adding endings (suffixes) to verbs.

1. If an ending begins with a consonant, it can usually be attached to the base word that ends in a consonant or a silent *e* with no change to the base word or the ending. For example, *ail* does not change when you add the ending *-ment* to make *ailment*.

2. If a base word ends in a silent *e* and the ending begins with a vowel, drop the silent *e* when adding the ending. With the word *strive*, for example, you would drop the silent *e* before adding the ending *-ing* to make *striving*.

3. When base words end in a consonant plus *-y* combination, change the *-y* to an *-i* when adding endings. The word *silly*, for instance, would become *sillier* and *silliest*. If the base word ends in a vowel-plus-*y* combination, keep the final *y*. For example, you would keep the final *y* when adding endings to the word *play*. In this case *play* would become *playing*, *played*, *plays*.

4. When a one-syllable base word ends in a consonant-plus-vowel-plus-consonant combination, double the final consonant when adding an ending that begins with a vowel. An example of this type of word is *span*. When adding endings such as *-ing* or *-ed*, you would double the final consonant to make *spanning* and *spanned*.

5. When a base word of more than one syllable ends in a consonant-plus-vowel-plus-consonant combination and the accent is on the final syllable, double the final consonant when adding an ending that begins with a vowel. This tip may sound a little confusing! An example of a multiple-syllable word ending in the consonant-plus-vowel-plus-consonant combination is *prefer*. You would double the final consonant when adding endings to *prefer* to make *preferring* and *preferred*.

6. When a base word ends in any other combination of vowels and consonants, do not double the final consonant when adding an ending. For example, you would not double the final consonant when adding endings to the word *ring*.

Future Tense

The future tense indicates future action (action that hasn't happened yet, but will).

> Brady *will ski* with us this week.

The future tense is formed by combining *will* with the present tense of the verb.

PROGRESSIVE

The progressive category is comprised of the present progressive tense, the past progressive tense, and the future progressive tense.

Present Progressive Tense

The present progressive tense indicates action that is in progress (action that is happening). The present progressive is formed by combining *am, is,* or *are* with the *-ing* form of the verb.

> They *are watching* "American Idol."

Keep the rules for adding endings to words in mind when forming the progressive tenses. It is important to note that you must drop a final *-e* before adding *-ing* to form the present participle (a present participle is used with the verb *to be*, to indicate an action that is ongoing; for example, *shine* becomes *is shining*).

Past Progressive Tense

The past progressive tense indicates action that was occurring at some specific time in the past.

> Abbie *was ordering* a milk shake.

The past progressive is formed by combining *was* or *were* with the *-ing* form of the verb.

Future Progressive Tense

The future progressive tense indicates action that is continuous or will occur in the future.

> Claire *will be playing* lacrosse this spring.

The future progressive is formed by combining *will be* with the *-ing* form of the verb.

....

TIP: The past-participle form of a verb is usually the simple past form of the verb: verb + *-ed*. This is the case with regular verbs. For example, *stop* becomes *stopped*, *talk* becomes *talked*, and *wash* becomes *washed*. With irregular verbs, however, this is not always the case. For example, *run* becomes *ran* (not *runned*) and *drink* becomes *drank* (not *drinked*). Irregular verbs are covered in Lesson 10.

Remember, some verbs double the final consonant or drop a final *y* or *e* when endings like *-d* and *-ed* are added.

....

PERFECT

The perfect category is comprised of the present perfect tense, the past perfect tense, and the future perfect tense.

Present Perfect Tense

The present perfect tense indicates that the action started some time in the past and is still going on.

> Hannah *has cleaned* her room all day.

The present perfect is formed by combining the helping verb *have* or *has* with the past-participle form of the verb. Keep the rules for adding endings to verbs in mind when forming this tense!

Past Perfect Tense

The past perfect tense indicates action that occurred some time in the past before another action began.

> Katie *had returned* her books to the library before Ashley asked to borrow them.

Much like the present-perfect form, the past perfect is formed by combining the helping verb *had* with the past participle form of the verb. Helping verbs let you know when the action of a verb takes place.

Future Perfect Tense

The future perfect tense indicates action that will occur and finish in the future before another action begins.

> Ethan *will have attended* soccer camp before the start of the fall season.

The future perfect tense is formed by combining the helping verbs *will have,* *would have,* or *will have been* with the past-participle form of the verb.

PRACTICE

Write the correct form of the verb in each of the following sentences.

1. My dad _____ me off at school today. (*to drop*: past tense)

2. I usually _____ for two hours every night. (*to study*: present tense)

3. The lion _____ on smaller animals. (*to prey*: past tense)

4. All of our vegetables _____ by the end of October. (*to harvest*: future perfect tense)

5. Tyler _____ at Mt. Snow tomorrow. (*to ski: future progressive tense*)

Conjugate each verb by writing the correct tense forms in the charts.

6. to tap

	Simple	Progressive	Perfect
Present	_____	_____	_____
Past	_____	_____	_____
Future	_____	_____	_____

7. to close

	Simple	Progressive	Perfect
Present	_____	_____	_____
Past	_____	_____	_____
Future	_____	_____	_____

8. to reply

	Simple	Progressive	Perfect
Present	_____	_____	_____
Past	_____	_____	_____
Future	_____	_____	_____

9. to hope

	Simple	Progressive	Perfect
Present	_____	_____	_____
Past	_____	_____	_____
Future	_____	_____	_____

10. to plan

	Simple	Progressive	Perfect
Present	_____	_____	_____
Past	_____	_____	_____
Future	_____	_____	_____

11. to concern

	Simple	Progressive	Perfect
Present	_____	_____	_____
Past	_____	_____	_____
Future	_____	_____	_____

12. to type

	Simple	Progressive	Perfect
Present	_____	_____	_____
Past	_____	_____	_____
Future	_____	_____	_____

13. to stare

	Simple	Progressive	Perfect
Present	_____	_____	_____
Past	_____	_____	_____
Future	_____	_____	_____

14. to refer

	Simple	Progressive	Perfect
Present	_____	_____	_____
Past	_____	_____	_____
Future	_____	_____	_____

15. to employ

	Simple	Progressive	Perfect
Present	_____	_____	_____
Past	_____	_____	_____
Future	_____	_____	_____

ANSWERS

1. My dad *dropped* me off at school today.

2. I usually *study* for two hours every night.

3. The lion *preyed* on smaller animals.

4. All of our vegetables *will be harvested* by the end of October.

5. Tyler *will be skiing* at Mt. Snow tomorrow.

6. to tap

	Simple	Progressive	Perfect
Present	tap	am/is/are tapping	have/has tapped
Past	tapped	was/were tapping	had tapped
Future	will tap	will be tapping	will have tapped

7. to close

	Simple	Progressive	Perfect
Present	close	am/is/are closing	have/has closed
Past	closed	was/were closing	had closed
Future	will close	will be closing	will have closed

8. to reply

	Simple	Progressive	Perfect
Present	reply	am/is/are replying	have/has replied
Past	replied	was/were replying	had replied
Future	will reply	will be replying	will have replied

9. to hope

	Simple	Progressive	Perfect
Present	hope	am/is/are hoping	have/has hoped
Past	hoped	was/were hoping	had hoped
Future	will hope	will be hoping	will have hoped

10. to plan

	Simple	Progressive	Perfect
Present	plan	am/is/are planning	have/has planned
Past	planned	was/were planning	had planned
Future	will plan	will be planning	will have planned

11. to concern

	Simple	Progressive	Perfect
Present	concern	am/is/are concerning	have/has concerned
Past	concerned	was/were concerning	had concerned
Future	will concern	will be concerning	will have concerned

12. to type

	Simple	Progressive	Perfect
Present	type	am/is/are typing	have/has typed
Past	typed	was/were typing	had typed
Future	will type	will be typing	will have typed

13. to stare

	Simple	Progressive	Perfect
Present	stare	am/is/are staring	have/has stared
Past	stared	was/were staring	had stared
Future	will stare	will be staring	will have stared

14. to refer

	Simple	**Progressive**	**Perfect**
Present	refer	am / is / are referring	have / has referred
Past	referred	was / were referring	had referred
Future	will refer	will be referring	will have referred

15. to employ

	Simple	**Progressive**	**Perfect**
Present	employ	am / is / are employing	have / has employed
Past	employed	was / were employing	had employed
Future	will employ	will be employing	will have employed

irregular verbs

He who controls the present, controls the past.
He who controls the past, controls the future.
—GEORGE ORWELL (1903–1950)
ENGLISH AUTHOR

As you learned in Lesson 9, regular verbs have a variety of tenses. The same is true of irregular verbs. In this lesson, you will learn what irregular verbs are and how you can best remember the correct ways to form them.

NOW THAT YOU understand the various verb tenses and how regular verbs are conjugated, let's look at the irregular verbs. With regular verbs, which comprise the majority of verbs in the English language, you can add *-ed* to the end of the word with little or no change (aside from some words that require you to double the final consonant or only add *-d* to words already ending in *-e*). With irregular verbs, however, that is not the case. Irregular verbs are words that don't follow a predictable pattern, like adding *-ed* to form the past tense. Unfortunately, for people who like to follow rules closely, there are many irregular verbs in the English language. The only way to learn the conjugation of these verbs into tenses is to memorize them.

COMMON IRREGULAR VERBS

The following chart shows the conjugation of most common irregular verbs. Don't let yourself be intimidated by the number of verbs that are irregular. The more you look at the list, the more you'll realize that you are already very familiar with many of these words and their spellings. In fact, for many people, this list will simply serve as a reminder of how the verbs are spelled.

As you read through the list, take note of words whose spelling does not make sense to you, or with which you are not familiar. Highlight those words and either add them to your spelling list or create flash cards based on them.

The chart groups the irregular verbs together based on the patterns they follow when forming the past tense and the past participle.

VERBS WITH NO CHANGE

Base	Past Tense	Past Participle
bet	bet	bet
bid	bid	bid
broadcast	broadcast	broadcast
burst	burst	burst
cast	cast	cast
cost	cost	cost
cut	cut	cut
forecast	forecast	forecast
hit	hit	hit
hurt	hurt	hurt
let	let	let
proofread	proofread	proofread
put	put	put
quit	quit	quit
shut	shut	shut
slit	slit	slit
split	split	split
spread	spread	spread
thrust	thrust	thrust
upset	upset	upset

VERBS WITH THE SAME PAST TENSE AND PAST PARTICIPLE

Base	Past Tense	Past Participle
bend	bent	bent
bind	bound	bound
bleed	bled	bled
breed	bred	bred
bring	brought	brought
build	built	built
buy	bought	bought
catch	caught	caught
cling	clung	clung
creep	crept	crept
dig	dug	dug
flee	fled	fled
fling	flung	flung
foretell	foretold	foretold
grind	ground	ground
hang	hung	hung
hold	held	held
keep	kept	kept
lead	led	led
lend	lent	lent
mean	meant	meant
mislay	mislaid	mislaid
shoot	shot	shot
slide	slid	slid
smell	smelled	smelled
speed	sped	sped
spin	spun	spun
string	strung	strung
stick	stuck	stuck
sting	stung	stung
sweep	swept	swept

weep	wept	wept
win	won	won
wind	wound	wound
wring	wrung	wrung

VERBS WITH THE SAME BASE AND PAST PARTICIPLE

Base	Past Tense	Past Participle
become	became	become
come	came	come
run	ran	run

VERBS WITH A PAST PARTICIPLE THAT ENDS IN -*N* OR -*EN*

Base	Past Tense	Past Participle
arise	arose	arisen
awake	awoke	awoken
beat	beat	beaten
bite	bit	bitten
draw	drew	drawn
fall	fell	fallen
forsake	forsook	forsaken
freeze	froze	frozen
get	got	gotten
hide	hid	hidden
know	knew	known
mistake	mistook	mistaken
overtake	overtook	overtaken
strew	strewed	strewn
strive	strove	striven
swear	swore	sworn
undertake	undertook	undertaken
wear	wore	worn
withdraw	withdrew	withdrawn
write	wrote	written

VERBS WITH MORE THAN ONE ACCEPTABLE PAST TENSE
AND/OR PAST PARTICIPLE FORM

Base	Past Tense	Past Participle
bear	bore	borne *or* born
dream	dreamed *or* dreamt	dreamed *or* dreamt
knit	knit *or* knitted	knit *or* knitted
lean	leaned *or* leant	leaned *or* leant
leap	leaped *or* leapt	leaped *or* leapt
learn	learned *or* leant	learned *or* learnt
prove	proved	proved *or* proven
rid	rid *or* ridded	rid *or* ridded
saw	sawed	sawed *or* sawn
sew	sewed	sewn *or* sewed
shave	shaved	shaved *or* shaven
shear	sheared	sheared *or* shorn
show	showed	showed *or* shown
sneak	sneaked *or* snuck	sneaked *or* snuck
spell	spelled *or* spelt	spelled *or* spelt
spill	spilled *or* spilt	spilled *or* spilt
spit	spat *or* spit	spat *or* spit
spoil	spoiled *or* spoilt	spoiled *or* spoilt
stink	stank *or* stunk	stunk
strike	struck	struck *or* stricken
swell	swelled	swelled *or* swollen
weave	wove *or* weaved	woven *or* weaved

VERBS WITH AN *I* THAT BECOMES AN *A* IN THE PAST TENSE
AND A *U* IN THE PAST PARTICIPLE

Base	Past Tense	Past Participle
drink	drank	drunk
ring	rang	rung
sing	sang	sung
shrink	shrank	shrunk
sink	sank	sunk
swim	swam	swum

VERBS WITH NO PATTERN

Base	Past Tense	Past Participle
do	did	done
go	went	gone
lie	lay	lain
light	lit	lighted
slay	slew	slain
undergo	underwent	undergone

TIP: Watch out for the verb *to be*, which is conjugated unlike any other verb. It is the only verb in the English language with an infinitive that differs from the present tense form. The infinitive is *to be* while the present tense is *am*, *is*, or *are*. So you would say:

> I *am* hungry. (first person singular)
> We *are* hungry. (first person plural)
> You *are* hungry. (second person)
> He (or she) *is* hungry. (third person singular)
> They *are* hungry. (third person plural)

The past tense and past participle forms are even trickier. The past tense of *to be* is *was* or *were*. The past participle form is *been*. For these forms, you would say:

> I *was* hungry. I *had been* hungry. (first person singular)
> We *were* hungry. We *had been* hungry. (first person plural)
> You *were* hungry. You *had been* hungry. (second person singular)

He (or she) *was* hungry. He (or she) *had been* hungry. (third person singular)

They *were* hungry. They *had been* hungry. (third person plural)

To be is the most common verb in the English language. But because it is confusing to conjugate, it is often misused. Memorizing the tenses of *to be* will help you improve not only your spelling but your grammar as well.

PRACTICE

Correct the **boldfaced** verbs in the following sentences, as necessary.

1. Marisol **feeled** sick to her stomach so she went home early.

2. I was afraid that the milk had **spoilt** from sitting on the counter this morning.

3. She **lent** her sister nine dollars.

4. Everyone was happy when Lisa **brang** cookies to practice.

5. Owen **betted** on the winner of the Kentucky Derby.

6. Brandon **heared** every word his mother said.

7. They had **blewn** up all the balloons.

8. Kelsey **won** first place in the spelling bee.

9. They spent an hour cleaning up after everyone **leaved**.

10. She was **forbidded** from going out after dark.

11. He took the time to thank his grandmother for the gift she **gived** him.

12. Lucy wondered who **tored** the pages out of her journal.

13. They **drank** all of the lemonade in the pitcher.

14. Tara asked her friends to tell her who **throwed** out her lunch tray.

15. The telephone **ringed** all afternoon.

ANSWERS

1. Marisol **felt** sick to her stomach so she went home early.

2. I was afraid that the milk had **spoiled** from sitting on the counter this morning. (**spoilt** would also be acceptable)

3. She **lent** her sister nine dollars. (**lent** is correct)

4. Everyone was happy when Lisa **brought** cookies to practice.

5. Owen **bet** on the winner of the Kentucky Derby.

6. Brandon **heard** every word his mother said.

7. They had **blown** up all the balloons.

8. Kelsey **won** first place in the spelling bee. (**won** is correct)

9. They spent an hour cleaning up after everyone **left**.

10. She was **forbidden** from going out after dark.

11. He took the time to thank his grandmother for the gift she **gave** him.

12. Lucy wondered who **tore** the pages out of her journal.

13. They **drank** all of the lemonade in the pitcher. (**drank** is correct)

14. Tara asked her friends to tell her who **threw** out her lunch tray.

15. The telephone **rang** all afternoon.

vowels

The English language is nobody's special property.
It is the property of the imagination:
it is the property of the language itself.
—DEREK WALCOTT (1930–)
ST. LUCIAN POET AND PLAYWRIGHT

Without vowels, we wouldn't have words. In this lesson, you'll learn about the long and short sounds that vowels make, along with the *schwa* and how to handle two-vowel combinations.

THE ALPHABET CONTAINS five vowels: *a, e, i, o,* and *u.* Although there are far fewer vowels than there are consonants, vowels are extremely important for forming words. In fact, they are so important that the consonant *y* is sometimes used as a vowel. That's because vowels are necessary for pronunciation. A vowel is defined as *a sound that is produced without blocking the passage of air from the throat.* In contrast, a consonant is a sound that is made by *blocking* the passage of air. In Lesson 14, you'll learn more about consonants and how they affect pronunciation. For now, suffice it to say that without both vowels and consonants, our words wouldn't make many sounds.

TIP: When you were learning vowels in school, you may have been taught the phrase *a, e, i, o, u, and sometimes y*. Although *y* is not officially a vowel, it is sometimes enlisted to serve as one. In those cases, the *y* makes the sound of a vowel; you might say that it is technically a vowel *in those cases*. For example, the words *why, my, hymn, lymph, sylph,* and *shy* don't contain one of the five vowels but they do contain a *y* that is making the sound of a vowel.

So, be sure to look out for *y* appearing in words without any other vowels. The letter *y* will undoubtedly be there making the sound of a vowel and that can throw you off (spelling *lymph*, for example, as *limph*).

VOWEL SOUNDS

Since there are only a handful of vowels, they work extra hard and make two types of sounds: short and long. Think about the five vowels and the sounds they make. If you pronounce words slowly, you'll notice that the vowels make different sounds. The letter *a*, for example, makes one sound in the words *game* and *late* and another sound in the words *cat* and *lack*. In the first pair of words, the sound is a long *a* and in the second pair, it is a short *a*. We use the terms short and long to describe the length of time the vowel sounds spend in the throat. A short *a* spends less time being sounded than a long *a*. The following list gives some examples of words with long and short vowels. (Remember, long vowels also make the same sound as the name of the vowel.)

Short Vowels	Long Vowels
acid	game
rat	tame
felt	scene
set	flight
bit	pine
wig	hone
hog	muse
monster	unify
rug	
tumble	

THE SCHWA

The schwa is a vowel sound that is neither short nor long; it can be made by any of the vowels. Because all vowels can make the schwa sound, it is the root of many spelling errors. The schwa is defined as *an unstressed and toneless vowel sound*. The dictionary shows it as an upside-down *e*; like this: ə. Words that contain the schwa include *fir*, *major*, *butter*, *burr*, *calendar*, *about*, *the*, *pencil*, *bishop*, *supply*, *adult*. As you can see from that list of words, the schwa makes a kind of *uh* sound, and all the vowels can represent it.

Since all the vowels can make the same schwa sound, you cannot rely on pronunciation to guide you with spelling words that contain the schwa. Instead, you will need to memorize the words. In some instances, you can rely on your knowledge of prefixes and suffixes to guide you. Knowing how to spell suffixes containing the schwa will help you to spell words that contain them correctly. Still, most words that contain the schwa sound—like many words in the English language—require you to memorize, plain and simple.

VOWEL COMBINATIONS

In Lesson 2, we touched on a mnemonic that is helpful for learning vowel combinations:

- When two vowels go walking, the first one does the talking.

This handy mnemonic helps you to remember which letter to write first in two-vowel combinations. In words with two-vowel combinations, the first vowel usually will be pronounced with a long vowel sound, while the second one will remain silent. If you know that a particular word has a vowel combination, but you aren't sure which vowel comes first and which one comes second, this rule can be useful. Following the rule, you would pronounce the word *brain*, for example, and by hearing that the long *a* is pronounced, but not the *i*, you would know to spell the word using the *ai* combination.

Here are a few examples of words with two-vowel combinations that contain either a long *a*, *e*, *i*, *o*, or *u* sound:

chaise

train

sustain

bean

peek

dic

roast

moat

woe

cue

suit

ruin

PRACTICE

Choose the correct spelling of each of the following words:

1. piasley / paisley

2. jiuce / juice

3. nuisance / niusance

4. concael / conceal

5. previal / prevail

6. refrian / refrain

7. menial / menail

8. certian / certain

9. draery / dreary

10. mountian / mountain

11. pryde / pride

12. shy / shi

13. lynx / linx

14. wicker / wycker

15. tryed / tried

16. dynamic / dinamic

17. myth / mith

18. cript / crypt

19. sygh / sigh

20. whine / whyne

21. foundation / fuondation

22. awthority / authority

23. duaghter / daughter

24. biosterous / boisterous

25. caution / cuation

ANSWERS

1. paisley
2. juice
3. nuisance
4. conceal
5. prevail
6. refrain
7. menial
8. certain
9. dreary
10. mountain
11. pride
12. shy
13. lynx
14. wicker
15. tried
16. dynamic
17. myth
18. crypt
19. sigh
20. whine
21. foundation
22. authority
23. daughter
24. boisterous
25. caution

using *ie* and *ei*

*Words differently arranged have a different meaning, and
meanings differently arranged have a different effect.*
—BLAISE PASCAL (1623–1662)
FRENCH PHILOSOPHER, MATHEMATICIAN, AND PHYSICIST

The vowel combination of *i* and *e* is a cause of frequent spelling errors. This lesson will explain when to use *ie* and when to use *ei*.

AS WE COVERED in Lesson 2, there is a clever mnemonic that outlines how and when to use the vowel combinations of *ie* and *ei*:

- *i* before *e*, except after *c* or when sounding like *-ay* as in *neighbor* or *weigh*.

This mnemonic covers the rule fairly well. There are, of course, some exceptions to the rule, which we will cover in this lesson. But first, let's review the basic rule. In most words that have the letters *i* and *e* grouped together to produce a long *e* sound, the *i* will come before the *e*. This holds true except for words having a *c* immediately before this combination. For example, in the words *piece* and *lien*, the *i* comes before the *e*. In the words *conceit* and *receive,* the *e* comes before the *i* because the combination is preceded by a *c*.

In words where the *i* and *e* combination produce the sound *-ay* (as in *neighbor* or *weigh* from the mnemonic), the order is reversed. Other examples are *reign, rein, beige,* and *vein.*

Now, the exceptions. There are a few words that do not follow this rule at all. Luckily, there is a mnemonic that can help you to remember the exceptions. In this case, the mnemonic is a silly sentence: *Neither leisure foreigner seized the weird heights, either.* All of the words in that sentence—except for *the*—are exceptions to the rule. That sentence might just be strange enough to stick in your head and to help you remember the exceptions! If not, you will have to memorize the words, because if you try to spell them according to the *ie* / *ei* rules, you will end up spelling them incorrectly.

PRACTICE

Unscramble the words below to find the answer to the puzzle.

Ava waited for the bus with her __ __ __ __ __ __ __ __ , Ryan.

1. O R I E F N G   __ __ __ __ __ __◯

2. E I C T R E P   __ __ __◯__ __ __

3. N C E E I   __◯__ __ __

4. N R I E G   __ __ __◯__

5. G H E H I T   ◯__ __ __ __ __

6. E B E G I   ◯__ __ __ __

7. C E C I V N O E   __◯__ __ __ __ __ __

8. U R L I S E E   __ __ __ __ __◯__

ANSWERS

1. foreign
2. receipt
3. niece
4. reign
5. height
6. beige
7. conceive
8. leisure

Ava waited for the bus with her **N E I G H B O R** , Ryan.

1. ORIEFNG   F O R E I G (N)

2. EICTREP   R E C (E) I P T

3. NCEEI   N (I) E C E

4. NRIEG   R E I (G) N

5. GHEHIT   (H) E I G H T

6. EBEGI   (B) E I G E

7. CECIVNOE   C (O) N C E I V E

8. URLISEE   L E I S U (R) E

using *ia* and *ai*

*Language is the most imperfect and expensive means yet
discovered for communicating thought.*

—WILLIAM JAMES (1842–1910)

AMERICAN PHILOSOPHER AND PSYCHOLOGIST

Another tricky vowel combination that tends to cause spelling errors is *ai / ia*.
This lesson will show you when to use each of these combinations.

MUCH AS WITH the *ie / ei* vowel combinations, the combination of *ai* or *ia* can
be confusing. If you reverse the correct order of the vowel combinations, you
will end up with an incorrectly spelled word. But there is an easy way to
remember when to use *ai* and when to use *ia*. In fact, if you are tired of rules that
seem complicated or full of exceptions, you are in luck with the rules for this
vowel combination.

The rules for using *ai* and *ia* are simple: There are two situations when you
should use *ai* and two when you should use *ia*. You should use *ai*

1. when the vowel combination makes the *uh* sound. Words like *vil-
   lain, fountain,* and *captain* use the *ai* combination.
2. when the vowel combination makes a long *a* sound. Remember the
   mnemonic covered in Lesson 2: *When two vowels go walking, the first
   one does the talking.* With words that have the long *a* sound, the
   combination is always *ai* and not *ia*. Words like *train* and *abstain* use
   the *ai* combination.

You should use *ia*

1. when each vowel is pronounced separately. Words like *median*, *alleviate*, and *auxiliary* use the *ia* combination.
2. when you add the *-al* ending to certain words. When a word ends in *-y* and you need to add the suffix *-al*, you must first change the *-y* to an *-i* and then add *-al*. In those cases, you will use the *ia* vowel combination, regardless of pronunciation. The word *controversial* illustrates this rule. *Controversial* is formed from the word *controversy* and the suffix *-al*. When adding the suffix, you change the *y* to an *i* and add *-al*: *controversial*. Even though the two vowels are not pronounced separately, they appear in the order *ia* because the *i* is taking the place of a *y*.

As you can see, you need to think about pronunciation in order to determine proper spelling in most situations. If you pronounce words with the *ai* and *ia* combinations incorrectly, you could set yourself up to spell them incorrectly as well. Pay attention to how words are pronounced and you will be more likely to use *ai* and *ia* correctly.

....

TIP: Lesson 22 covers the final *y*—when to keep it and when to change it to *i*—in greater detail. Jump ahead to that lesson if you would like more information on the final *y*.

....

Here is a list of common words that use the two vowel combinations. As you read through the list, say each word out loud. Listen to how it sounds, and note whether it includes the *ai* or the *ia* combination. If you are unfamiliar with any words on the list, look them up in your dictionary and write out their meanings so you will know the words in the future.

ai Words	*ia* Words
abstain	alleviate
Britain	artificial
captain	auxiliary
certain	congenial
chaise	controversial

ai Words	*ia* Words
contain	familiar
curtain	guardian
detain	immediate
entertain	Indian
fountain	judicial
mountain	Martian
paisley	median
refrain	menial
restrain	pronunciation
sustain	substantial
train	
villain	

PRACTICE

The following paragraph contains several boldfaced words that contain the *ai* or the *ia* vowel combinations. Circle the words that are spelled incorrectly.

Zoe and Rory decided that they would look for jobs **immediately** after the school year ended. Unfortunately, they were not **familair** with the local job market. Most students spent a **substantial** amount of time looking for work before the end of the school year. By the time Zoe and Rory began their search, only **menial** jobs with a low **medain** starting hourly rate were left. The positions in the **judicail** area, where they had **entertained** hopes of working, had all been filled.

ANSWERS

The incorrectly spelled words are *familiar, median, judicial*; the vowel combination *ai* is used between consonants and is usually pronounced as a long *a*.

consonants

Language is not only the vehicle of thought, it is a
great and efficient instrument in thinking.
—Sir Humphrey Davy (1778–1829)
Cornish chemist and inventor

Although most consonants have only one pronunciation, there are six that can
be pronounced two or more ways. In this lesson you will learn about consonant
pronunciation, what the various sounds are, and how to remember the correct
spelling of tricky words, even when their pronunciation throws you off.

IN LESSON 3, you learned about pronunciation. Proper pronunciation is a key
to learning how to spell words correctly. Then, in Lesson 11, you learned about
vowels and the various ways they can be pronounced. With consonants, on the
other hand, while there is some variation based on letter combinations, the pronunciation is fairly consistent and straightforward.

There are a few exceptions to this generalization. For example, the letters
c and *g* can each be pronounced two different ways, soft or hard: *center, carton,
general, garden*. This characteristic can lead to faulty spelling. A soft *c* can be mistaken for an *s* and a hard *c* for a *k*. Let's take a look at what the soft and hard pronunciation means. But before we get into the anomalies of consonants, let's
review the basics.

Our alphabet contains 21 consonants, and almost all of them make the same
sound all the time. Six of those consonants can make more than one sound,

however: *c, g, q, s, x,* and *y*. In pronunciation, consonant sounds are created by blocking the flow of air from the throat using the lips or tongue. Six mouth positions are used to produce consonants; you can feel the different positions when you speak. Try reading parts of this lesson aloud, paying attention to how your tongue or lips move with each letter and sound. You will notice that each letter requires your mouth, lips, and tongue to move in certain predictable ways.

TIP: Here is a quick refresher on the sounds that each consonant makes.

b	**b**oy
c	pla**c**e, **c**ase
d	**d**og
f	e**f**fort
g	**g**ent, **g**ree
h	**h**ow
j	**j**ump
l	a**l**oud
m	**m**oney
n	**n**ail
p	**p**aid
q	**qu**ick, uni**qu**e
r	**r**ecord, supe**r**
s	**s**ound, tree**s**
t	i**t**em
v	**v**iolin
w	**w**elcome, a**w**e
x	a**x**, **x**ylophone, e**x**ist
z	**z**ip

Of the 21 consonants, there are only three—*c, q,* and *x*—that do not make their own unique sounds; that is, other letters can make the same sounds. The letter *c* can make two different sounds, both of which are also made by other letters. *C* can sound like *s*, as in *nice* and *advice*, or it can sound like *k*, as in *coward* and *cry*. To further complicate the issue, there are some words, such as *accent* and *succinct*, where *c* makes both sounds.

The letter *q* is another anomaly. In English, the letter *q* is almost invariably followed by the letter *u*. (The few words in the dictionary in which *q* is not followed by *u* are mostly words that have been borrowed from other languages.)

The English *q* + *u* combination can be pronounced either as *kw*, as in *queen*, or as *k*, as in *unique*.

Lastly, the letter *x* can represent three different sounds. When it appears at the beginning of a word, it usually sounds like a *z*, as in *xylophone*. When it follows the letter *e* at the beginning of a word it usually makes a *gs* sound, as in *exact*. In all other cases, *x* makes a *ks* sound, as in *box* or *taxi*.

SOFT AND HARD *C* AND *G*

The letters *c* and *g* can be pronounced in two distinct ways: soft or hard. A soft *c* is pronounced like an *s* and a hard *c* is pronounced like a *k*. A soft *g* is pronounced like a *j* and a hard *g* is pronounced with a *guh* sound. Two rules will help you to determine whether to pronounce these letters with a soft or a hard sound.

1. When the letter *c* or *g* is followed by an *e, i,* or *y,* it will almost always be soft.
2. When the letter *c* or *g* is followed by an *a, o,* or *u,* it will almost always be hard.
3. When the letter *c* or *g* is followed by a consonant, it will almost always be hard.

Let's look at some examples for each case.

Soft c (sounds like s)	Soft g (sounds like j)	Hard c (sounds like k)	Hard g (sounds like guh)
central	genius	case	gamble
circle	giant	cousin	gone
cymbal	gym	current	gumption
circus	gentleman	cloud	guess
cent	generous	carton	girl
		rectify	ragtime
		recluse	program

PRACTICE

Choose the correctly spelled *italicized* word in each of the following sentences.

1. In *jeneral* / *general*, she was pleased with the results.

2. The family liked to see the *giraffes* / *jiraffes* at the zoo.

3. Her New Year's resolution was to *join* / *goin* the *gim* / *gym*.

4. He bought a new pair of hedge *clippers* / *klippers*.

5. Harry became an actor because he loved to be the *senter* / *center* of attention.

6. My grandfather works *ceaselessly* / *seacelessly* even thought he's more than 80 years old.

7. Ms. Cooper is an account *egsecutive* / *executive* at the ad agency.

8. I need an *access* / *axess* code to get into my e-mail *ackount* / *account*.

9. They were not prepared for the pop *kwiz* / *quiz*.

10. The Smiths had a large eat-in *kitchen* / *citchen*.

11. *Ceveral* / *Several* kids were at the party last night.

12. I didn't think that movie made any *cense* / *sense*!

13. We learned about how dinosaurs came to be *extinct* / *ekstinct*.

14. That little car sure is *xippy* / *zippy*!

15. You can save money at the grocery store if you use *koupons* / *coupons*.

ANSWERS

1. In *general,* she was pleased with the results.

2. The family liked to see the *giraffes* at the zoo.

3. Her New Year's resolution was to *join* the *gym.*

4. He bought a new pair of hedge *clippers.*

5. Harry became an actor because he loved to be the *center* of attention.

6. My grandfather works *ceaselessly* even though he's more than 80 years old.

7. Ms. Cooper is an account *executive* at the ad agency.

8. I need an *access* code to get into my e-mail *account.*

9. They were not prepared for the pop *quiz.*

10. The Smiths had a large eat-in *kitchen.*

11. *Several* kids were at the party last night.

12. I didn't think that movie made any *sense*!

13. We learned about how dinosaurs came to be *extinct.*

14. That little car sure is *zippy*!

15. You can save money at the grocery store if you use *coupons.*

LESSON 15

consonant combinations

In this lesson you'll learn about consonant combinations and silent consonants, which have fewer rules than those you learned about in Lesson 14.

CONSONANT COMBINATIONS CAN BE very confusing. There are no hard-and-fast rules for the combinations. The best way to learn how to spell words with tricky combinations is to memorize them. There are ways to make the memorization easier, however.

DIGRAPHS AND TRIGRAPHS

Many consonant combinations—called *digraphs* and *trigraphs*— are pronounced as one sound. Digraphs are two-letter combinations and trigraphs are three-letter combinations pronounced as one sound. Let's take a look at the most common digraphs and trigraphs. The sound that each makes is noted in parentheses.

Digraphs			Trigraphs		
bb	(b)	e**bb**	dge	(j)	ple**dge**
bt	(t)	de**bt**	tch	(ch)	la**tch**
cc	(k)	a**cc**urate			
ch	(ch)	whi**ch**			
ck	(k)	spe**ck**			
ff	(f)	stu**ff**			
gg	(guh)	e**gg**			
gh	(w)	bou**gh**			
gh	(g)	**gh**ost			
gh	(f)	cou**gh**			
gn	(n)	**gn**ome			
kn	(n)	**kn**ow			
ll	(l)	ma**ll**			
mb	(m)	thu**mb**			
mm	(m)	cla**mm**y			
ng	(ng)	thi**ng**			
nk	(nk)	wi**nk**			
nn	(n)	wi**nn**er			
ph	(f)	**ph**one			
qu	(k)	cli**qu**e			
sh	(sh)	**sh**ift			
ss	(s)	cla**ss**			
th	(th)	**th**in			
tt	(t)	le**tt**er			
wh	(h)	**wh**o			
wh	(hw)	**wh**en			
wr	(r)	**wr**ong			

As you can see, some of these combinations create sounds that are quite different from the way they look. In fact, some of the combinations are pretty strange! The combination *mb*, for instance, can be tough to remember because the *b* is completely silent. A word like *plumbing* is often incorrectly spelled *plumming* for that very reason. Consonant combinations such as *sh* and *th* are easier to remember because there are no other letters or combinations that produce those sounds.

You can familiarize yourself with the most common consonant combinations by committing them to memory. Use the preceding list as a guide to memorize the combinations. Learning which combination makes a particular sound will help you to remember the correct spelling of the words that contain the tricky combinations.

CONSONANT BLENDS

In the previous set of consonant combinations, the two (or three) letters created one new sound. Another set of combinations, called consonant blends, keep the original sounds of each letter. Here is a list of the most common consonant blends; the blended sound that each makes is noted in parentheses.

bl	(bl)	**bl**end	sm	(sm)	**sm**art
br	(br)	**br**eak	sn	(sn)	**sn**ail
cl	(kl)	**cl**ean	sp	(sp)	**sp**ort
cr	(kr)	**cr**edit	st	(st)	**st**amp
dr	(dr)	**dr**ive	sw	(sw)	**sw**ing
fl	(fl)	**fl**ower	tr	(tr)	**tr**ick
fr	(fr)	**fr**iend	tw	(tw)	**tw**ist
gl	(gl)	**gl**ue	scr	(skr)	**scr**atch
gr	(gr)	**gr**een	shr	(shr)	**shr**ed
nd	(nd)	seco**nd**	spl	(spl)	**spl**ay
pl	(pl)	**pl**ace	spr	(spr)	**spr**ing
pr	(pr)	**pr**oud	squ	(skw)	**squ**are
sk	(sk)	**sk**etch	str	(str)	**str**aight
sl	(sl)	**sl**eep	thr	(thr)	**thr**ough

As you can see from the list, the sound of each letter blends with the other(s), as if the two (or three) letters were sliding together. This should make it easier for you to remember consonant blends than the other consonant combinations.

SILENT CONSONANTS

Sometimes a consonant appears in a combination but makes no sound. Most of these silent consonants do not follow consistent rules, which can make it difficult to spell the words that contain them. Since there are few tips and rules to define when silent consonants are used in words, it's best to memorize those words.

Some words contain silent letters because their pronunciation has morphed over years of usage. For example, the compound words *clapboard* and *cupboard* were both probably originally pronounced as they are spelled, but over the years, the pronunciation changed so that they are both pronounced with a silent *p*.

Sneaky silent consonants call for you to employ some memory tricks. Here is a list of common words that contain silent consonants. Each of the silent consonants is set in **boldface**. Practice this list of words using flash cards or by creating mnemonics to learn the tricky words.

ai**s**le	hand**s**ome	**p**sychology
althou**gh**	hi**gh**	ras**p**berry
ans**w**er	**h**onor	rei**g**n
autum**n**	indi**c**t	r**h**etorical
b**l**ight	is**l**and	r**h**yme
ca**l**f	**k**neel	sub**t**le
cas**t**le	**k**night	throu**gh**
cu**p**board	**k**nowledge	We**d**nesday
de**b**t	li**gh**t	woul**d**
dou**b**t	mor**t**gage	**w**restle
fei**g**n	neigh**b**or	**w**rite
ghost	**p**salm	**w**rong
gnat	**p**seudonym	ya**ch**t
gnaw		

PRACTICE

Unscramble the following words that contain consonant combinations.

1. F N A L K

2. G H T D O U R

3. S H S P L A

4. T H G H R U O

5. C D R W O

6. A S I E L

7. H A M E N D S O

8. G A S H N

9. A S T K

10. W I T R E

11. T A S M P

12. E N D L B

13. Q A R E U S

14. L A I N S D

15. T H M B U

ANSWERS

1. flank
2. drought
3. splash
4. through
5. crowd
6. aisle
7. handsome
8. gnash
9. task
10. write
11. stamp
12. blend
13. square
14. island
15. thumb

SECTION 3

punctuation

WHEN YOU THINK of punctuation marks, you might think only of the marks used in sentences—for instance, commas, colons, and periods. But there are punctuation marks that are used in words as well. Proper placement of the punctuation marks that are used in words is essential. If you misplace an apostrophe or a hyphen, you may be drastically changing the meaning of the word.

Apostrophes: The apostrophe is used to show possession and contraction. It is *not* used to form the plural of words.

Hyphens: A hyphen can join two or more words together or it can divide them. Hyphens are also used for writing out ranges of numbers.

apostrophes

In this lesson, you will learn the two uses for apostrophes—to make contractions and to show possession—and when and how to use them properly.

THE POOR APOSTROPHE. It is one of the most commonly misused punctuation marks, often showing up where it simply isn't needed. There are only two uses for apostrophes: to make a contraction and to show possession. Never use an apostrophe to form the plural of a word.

CONTRACTIONS

The word *contract* (pronounced with the stress on the second syllable: *con-TRACT*) means to press together or to shorten. *Contractions* are words formed by pressing two words together, dropping one or more letters, and putting an apostrophe in the place of the omitted letter(s). This last part is the key point for you to learn: In a contraction, an apostrophe takes the place of one or more dropped letters.

For example, the words *can* and *not* can be written as the contraction *can't*. In this case, the apostrophe takes the place of the dropped letters *n* and *o*. Contractions are freely used in speech and in informal writing, but are discouraged in formal writing.

···

TIP: A *contraction* is a word that has been shortened by dropping some of the letters. An apostrophe is used *in place of* the dropped letters, as in *didn't* (*did not*) and *they've* (*they have*).

···

CONTRACTIONS OF COMMON PRONOUNS

	am/are/is	will	have/has	had/would
I	I'm	I'll	I've	I'd
you	you're	you'll	you've	you'd
he	he's	he'll	he's	he'd
she	she's	she'll	she's	she'd
it	it's	it'll	it's	it'd
they	they're	they'll	they've	they'd
we	we're	we'll	we've	we'd

···

TIP: Never confuse *it's* with *its*. *It's* is a contraction of the words *it is* or *it has*. *Its* is the possessive form of the word *it*. Remember to use the apostrophe with the word *it* only when you can add the word *is* or *has*: *it is* or *it has* = *it's*.

···

CONTRACTIONS OF HELPING VERBS

is	+	not	=	isn't	might	+	not	=	mightn't
are	+	not	=	aren't	can	+	not	=	can't
was	+	not	=	wasn't	do	+	not	=	don't
were	+	not	=	weren't	did	+	not	=	didn't
have	+	not	=	haven't	could	+	not	=	couldn't
has	+	not	=	hasn't	should	+	not	=	shouldn't
had	+	not	=	hadn't	would	+	not	=	wouldn't

POSSESSIVES

A possessive noun indicates ownership of something by that person, place, or thing. The possessive is generally formed by adding an apostrophe and an *s* to the end of a word. Note the following rules (and exceptions!) for correctly signifying possession.

Singular noun: add *'s*

Alanna's orange kite

Alaska's state bird

the book's cover

Singular noun ending in *-ss*: add *'s*

the waitress's first shift

the hostess's home

Plural noun ending in *-s*: add *'*

the lawyers' bills

the Smiths' new house

Irregular plural noun not ending in *-s*: add *'s*

the children's toys

the women's clothing

Compound noun: add 's to the end of the final word

> my mother-in-law's house
> the maid of honor's gown

Joint possession: add 's to the end of the final name

> Jennifer and David's car
> Amy, Barbara, and Allison's trip

Separate possession: add 's to the end of both names

> Suzette's and Veronica's clothes
> Jane's and Lisa's sons

PRACTICE

Place apostrophes where they belong in the following sentences.

1. Were heading out to the beach for the afternoon.

2. Dont eat that cake; its for Connor!

3. Claires best friends name is Lauren.

4. One of her blouses buttons is missing.

5. Jeremy thinks that Im keeping secrets.

6. Couldnt we go to Jodis party this Friday?

7. We thought the movies plot was too confusing, even though were science fiction fans.

8. Be sure to check that the bikes tires are inflated properly.

9. Take off your boots if youve been outside in the snow.

10. Its too bad that the stuffed teddy bear has lost its fuzz.

ANSWERS

1. We're heading out to the beach for the afternoon.
2. Don't eat that cake; it's for Connor!
3. Claire's best friend's name is Lauren.
4. One of her blouse's buttons is missing.
5. Jeremy thinks that I'm keeping secrets.
6. Couldn't we go to Jodi's party this Friday?
7. We thought the movie's plot was too confusing, even though we're science fiction fans.
8. Be sure to check that the bike's tires are inflated properly.
9. Take off your boots if you've been outside in the snow.
10. It's too bad that the stuffed teddy bear has lost its fuzz.

hyphens

Think like a wise man but communicate in the language of the people.
—WILLIAM BUTLER YEATS (1865–1939)
IRISH POET AND DRAMATIST

This lesson will show you how to use hyphens to divide or join words so you can be sure to convey the correct meaning to your audience.

YOU CAN USE HYPHENS in many ways: to divide a word at the end of a line, to join numbers and some compound words, and to attach prefixes to other words. Keep in mind that although most prefixes are joined directly to words without the need for hyphens, there are instances when you will need to use a hyphen to add a prefix. Joining two or more words, however, often calls for the use of a hyphen, especially if the phrase will act as an adjective.

Here are a few quick rules that can help you remember when to use hyphens. You should always use a hyphen:

- when words are used together to describe family relationships or job titles: *sister-in-law, mother-in-law, editor-in-chief, sergeant-at-arms*
- when joining a prefix to a capitalized word: *post-World War II, un-American, Mid-Atlantic*
- when forming an adjective that appears before a noun: *first-rate hotel, five-star restaurant, well-built house,* but not when the adjective follows the noun: *the hotel was first rate*

- to form ethnic designations: *African-American, Chinese-American, Indo-European*
- to link certain prefixes, such as *vice-, ex-, great-, all-,* or *self-,* to base words: *vice-chancellor, ex-husband, great-grandfather, all-encompassing, self-employed*
- to link the suffix *-elect* to base words: *president-elect, chairman-elect*
- to write out fractions: *one-half, one-third, three-fourths*
- to write out the numbers from 21 to 99: *twenty-one* to *ninety-nine*
- to combine numbers with nouns: *fifty-cent ride, one-year term*
- to divide words at the end of a line of writing (here, words must be divided either at a syllable break or between double consonants: *ap-pear-ance, sim-pli-fy, re-frig-er-a-tor*)

TIP: All words have one or more *syllables,* or individual spoken units. To determine where the syllable breaks are in a word that you need to hyphenate at the end of a line, tap your finger or clap your hands for each spoken unit of the word. For example, let's take the word *impor-tant.* Tap as you say each syllable: *im* (tap) *por* (tap) *tant* (tap). The word has three syllables: *im-por-tant.* You can hyphenate *important* at either of the two syllable breaks: *im-portant* or *impor-tant.*

You can also use hyphens to form compound words whose spelling would otherwise appear awkward. For example, if you wanted to describe a set of buttons as looking like shells, you might say they were *shell-like.* Without the hyphen, the new word would have an awkward three *l*s in a row: *shelllike.* The hyphen makes the word easier to read and understand.

PRACTICE

Choose the correct word or phrase to complete each sentence.

1. Her *father-in-law* / *father in law* lives in Florida.

2. The depth of her depression was *unfathomable* / *un-fathomable* to her friends.

3. I am still on good terms with my *exsupervisor* / *ex-supervisor*.

4. Cindy is proud of her *Japanese-American* / *Japanese American* heritage.

5. Rhonda's brother was a *well-known* / *well known* restaurateur.

Write out the numbers listed below, using hyphens when necessary.

6. $\frac{9}{12}$

7. $\frac{1}{4}$

8. 543

9. 3,455

10. 12

Add hyphens as you would if these words appeared at the end of a line of writing (separate the words by syllables).

11. friendly

12. giggle

13. balloon

14. alphabet

15. baggage

ANSWERS

1. Her *father-in-law* lives in Florida.
2. The depth of her depression was *unfathomable* to her friends.
3. I am still on good terms with my *ex-supervisor*.
4. Cindy is proud of her *Japanese-American* heritage.
5. Rhonda's brother was a *well-known* restaurateur.
6. nine-twelfths

7. one-fourth
8. five hundred forty-three
9. three thousand four hundred fifty-five
10. twelve
11. friend-ly
12. gig-gle
13. bal-loon
14. al-pha-bet
15. bag-gage

capitalization

Write with nouns and verbs.
—WILLIAM STRUNK, JR. (1869–1946)
AMERICAN AUTHOR AND ENGLISH PROFESSOR

In addition to capitalizing words at the beginning of sentences, we capitalize other words only for very specific reasons. This lesson explains the rules for capitalizing words.

THE MOST COMMON use of capitalization is for the first word in a sentence. Other words that must be capitalized are proper nouns, proper adjectives, certain words in titles, and the first word in a direct quotation.

PROPER NOUNS

Unlike common nouns—general terms for people, places, or things, like *person, store, holiday, hospital, cat*—proper nouns are very specific. Examples of proper nouns are *Jennifer Aniston* (instead of *person*), *Target* (instead of *store*), *Thanksgiving* (instead of *holiday*), *Memorial Hospital* (instead of *hospital*), and *Rex* (instead of *cat*). All proper nouns are capitalized to signify their importance.

When writing about a person, you may often need to include a title (*Mr., Ms., Dr.*), an abbreviation that follows the name (*Jr., Sr., Esq.*), or an initial

(*M. Brian Gibbs, Julia L. Cohen, Aidan H. Walker*). All three of these items should always be capitalized.

....

TIP: Watch out for common overcapitalization errors! Do not capitalize *north*, *south*, *east*, and *west* (the cardinal directions) and *winter*, *spring*, *summer*, and *fall* (the four seasons) except when they are the first word of a sentence, when the direction refers to a specific part of the country (as in *the Northeast*), or when the words are part of a title (as in *Winter Ball*).

....

PROPER ADJECTIVES

A proper adjective is a proper noun acting like an adjective, providing more information about the person, place, or thing being described. Proper adjectives are always capitalized, for example, *French toast*, *Greek olives*, or *April showers*.

TITLES

Many of the words in the title of a work such as a book, play, or movie are capitalized. The first word, of course, always requires capitalization. So, too, do all nouns, personal pronouns, verbs, and key words. Articles (such as, *a*, *an*, and *the*), conjunctions (*for, so, and, but, nor, or,* and *yet*), and prepositions (*to, beyond, under,* and so on) are not capitalized. Here are some examples of capitalization in titles.

Books	*The Little Prince*
Newspapers	*The New York Times*
Magazines	*Runner's World*
Short Stories	"The Lottery"
Paintings	*The Girl with the Pearl Earring*
Songs	"Mary Had a Little Lamb"
Movies	*Nick and Norah's Infinite Playlist*

TIP: Titles of books, works of art, movies, aircraft, and ships are underlined or italicized. Titles of short stories and songs (works that are often published within other works) are enclosed within quotation marks.

QUOTATIONS

The first word in a direct quotation (a person's exact spoken words) is always capitalized. For example:

At the meeting, John said, "The new routing software has made my job so much easier."

The first word after a quotation mark is not capitalized, however, when the quotation is continued after an interrupter (such as *he said* or *she replied*).

"Now," John continued, "our department runs much more smoothly and efficiently."

PRACTICE

Which words should be capitalized in the following sentences?

1. *seven pounds* is will smith's new movie.

2. allison and matt enjoyed watching their daughter, maeve, play basketball.

3. albany is the capital of new york state.

4. most of the kids wanted to eat hamburgers instead of the italian subs.

5. Emily won tickets to see the new york yankees in the world series.

6. it has been a year since louise lost her job at the carter, fink law firm.

7. april showers bring may flowers.

8. barack obama is our 44th president.

9. the piano teacher started the lesson with "row, row, row your boat."

10. john's mother was very curious about his facebook page.

ANSWERS

1. *Seven Pounds* is Will Smith's new movie.
2. Allison and Matt enjoyed watching their daughter, Maeve, play basketball.
3. Albany is the capital of New York State.
4. Most of the kids wanted to eat hamburgers instead of the Italian subs.
5. Emily won tickets to see the New York Yankees in the World Series.
6. It has been a year since Louise lost her job at the Carter, Fink law firm.
7. April showers bring May flowers.
8. Barack Obama is our 44th president.
9. The piano teacher started the lesson with "Row, Row, Row Your Boat."
10. John's mother was very curious about his Facebook page.

abbreviations and acronyms

Do not accustom yourself to use big words for little matters.
—SAMUEL JOHNSON (1709–1784)
ENGLISH AUTHOR

Reviewing the lists in this lesson will help you to understand the proper use of the most common abbreviations and acronyms in your writing.

AN ABBREVIATION IS a shortened form of a word or phrase; it is pronounced exactly the same as the full word. For example, the abbreviation *Dr.* is pronounced *doctor* and the abbreviation *Assn.* is pronounced *association.*

Most abbreviations are followed by periods except in these cases:

- two-letter postal code abbreviations for states
- initials representing a company, agency, or other business
- letters in acronyms
- the words hour, minute, and second

An acronym is formed from the first letters of a name, such as *SPAC* for *Saratoga Performing Arts Center.* It can also be formed by combining the first letters of parts of a series of words, such as *radar* for *ra*dio *d*etecting *a*nd *r*anging. Unlike abbreviations, acronyms are not followed by periods. And they are usually pronounced the way they look. For instance, you would say *radar*, not *radio detecting and ranging*.

Learning the most common abbreviations and acronyms will help you understand how they are created, and what is and is not a correct abbreviation or acronym. In general, words are abbreviated by maintaining the key letters that make the new word recognizable as a shortened version of the full one. Review the following lists to improve your knowledge of abbreviations and acronyms.

ABBREVIATIONS AND ACRONYMS

Clock and Calendar

days of the week: Sun., Mon., Tues., Wed., Thurs., Fri., Sat.

months of the year: Jan., Feb., Mar., Apr., May (no abbreviation), Jun., Jul., Aug., Sept., Oct., Nov., Dec.

A.D. = anno Domini

B.C. = before Christ

B.C.E. = before the common era

A.M. = ante meridiem (before noon)

P.M. = post meridiem (after noon) (a.m. and p.m. are exception to the no-period-for-acronyms rule)

CST = Central Standard Time

DST = Daylight Saving Time

EST = Eastern Standard Time

MST = Mountain Standard Time

PST = Pacific Standard Time

c. = circa (approximate date)

hr. = hour

min. = minute

sec. = second

mo. = month

yr. = year

Directions and Addresses

Apt. = apartment

Ave. = avenue

Blvd. = boulevard

Cir. = circle

Ct. = court

Dr. = drive (note that this is the same abbreviation as for doctor)

Ln. = lane

Rd. = road

St. = street

Ste. = suite

Ter. = terrace

Tpk. = turnpike

E = east

N = north

S = south

W = west

U.S.A. = United States of America

Acad. = academy

Assn. = association

Corp. = corporation

Dept. = department

Div. = division

Ft. = fort

Univ. = university

Personal Titles

Capt. = captain

Col. = colonel

Cpl. = corporal

Gen. = general

Lt. = lieutenant

Sgt. = sergeant

Dr. = doctor

L.P.N. = licensed practical nurse

R.N. = registered nurse

Esq. = esquire

Gov. = governor

Mr. = mister

Mrs. = missus

Ms. = miz

Prof. = professor

Msgr. = monsignor

Sr. = sister

Jr. = junior

Sr. = senior

Academic Degrees

B.A. = bachelor of arts

B.B.A. = bachelor of business administration

B.S. = bachelor of science

D.A. = doctor of arts

Ed.D. = doctor of education

J.D. = doctor of law

M.A. = master of arts

M.B.A. = master of business administration

M.D. = doctor of medicine

M.S. = master of science

Ph.D. = doctor of philosophy

Miscellaneous Others

AKA = also known as

ASAP = as soon as possible (sometimes pronounced *ay-say*)

ATM = automated teller machine

ID = identification

IQ = intelligence quotient

MC = master of ceremonies (sometimes written out as *emcee*)

PIN = personal identification number

P.S. = postscript

RSVP = *respondez s'il vous plaît* (French for *please reply*)

SPF = sun protection factor

TBA = to be announced

TBD = to be determined

PRACTICE

Select the correct abbreviation or acronym to replace the underlined words in each sentence.

1. Mary-Louise was working toward her <u>Bachelor of Arts</u> degree.
   a. BoA
   b. Bas
   c. B.A.
   d. b.a.

2. When Kim Jones, <u>Esquire</u>, started at the law firm, her name was engraved on the door.
   a. Eqr.
   b. Eqe.
   c. Esq.
   d. Esr.

3. His new address was 1 Sycamore <u>Lane</u>.
    a. Ln.
    b. Le.
    c. La.
    d. ln.

4. His old address was 22 Whitehall <u>Turnpike</u>.
    a. tpke.
    b. Trk.
    c. Tnpk.
    d. Tpk.

5. <u>Monsignor</u> Kelly was not available for Veronica's wedding.
    a. Mon.
    b. Mnr.
    c. Msgr.
    d. Msg.

6. Can we schedule the meeting for <u>Thursday</u>?
    a. Th.
    b. Thurs.
    c. Thur.
    d. Thy.

7. School will start again in <u>September</u>.
    a. Sep.
    b. Spt.
    c. Sept.
    d. Sptr.

8. Allison's father had a <u>Doctor of Philosophy</u> degree in English.
    a. Ph.D.
    b. PHD.
    c. PhD
    d. DPh

9. Mr. Lewis' birth was listed as <u>circa</u> 1890.

    a. ca.

    b. cir.

    c. c.

    d. C.

10. Kelsey was trying to complete her report <u>as soon as possible</u>.

    a. A.S.A.P.

    b. asap

    c. ASAP.

    d. ASAP

ANSWERS

1. c. B.A.

2. c. Esq.

3. a. Ln.

4. d. Tpk.

5. c. Msgr.

6. b. Thurs.

7. c. Sept.

8. a. Ph.D.

9. c. c.

10. d. ASAP

S E C T I O N 4

word endings

ENDINGS ARE ADDED to words to make them plural or to change their form. Many rules govern how endings can be added to words and, of course, there are many exceptions to those rules. Some words require that letters be dropped when adding endings, some require that letters be added, and some require major changes. The lessons in this section will cover how to form regular and irregular plurals, when to keep a final *e* and when to drop it, when to keep a final *y* and when to change it to an *i*, and when to double a final consonant.

regular plurals

By such innovations are languages enriched, when the words are adopted by the multitude, and naturalized by custom.
—MIGUEL DE CERVANTES SAAVEDRA (1547–1616)
SPANISH NOVELIST, POET, AND PLAYWRIGHT

Many words have regular plurals: you only have to add *-s* or *-es* to make them plural. This lesson will outline the rules for regular plurals.

WHEN WE TALK about plurals, we are referring to nouns that show more than one thing. A plural can mean two *dogs* (the plural of *dog*) or 1,000 *dogs*. The key is that the plural form indicates more than one *dog*. When you write about more than one of something, you need to use the plural form of the word.

There are two types of plurals in the English language: regular plurals and irregular plurals. Regular plurals are words that require only the addition of *-s* or *-es* at the end to make them plural. The rules for regular plurals are very straightforward. Irregular plurals, on the other hand, follow more complicated rules; they are covered in Lesson 21. Here, we'll review the rules for regular plurals which, fortunately, make up the majority of all plurals.

MOST WORDS

Most words only require you to add *-s* to the end. In fact, you can simply add *-s* to all words except for those that require *es* and those that are irregular.

WORDS THAT END IN -s, -x, -z, -ch, -sh

Add -es to words that end in -s, -x, -z, -ch, or -sh. The reason -es is added to words ending in these letters or letter combinations is that it makes them easier to pronounce. You'll notice that all the letters and letter combinations have similar, hissing-type sounds. If you were to simply add an -s at the end of these words, the sound of it would be lost. For example, it would be difficult to hear an -s at the end of the word *wax*. When -es is added, however, it becomes noticeable. The same is true for words that end in -ch or -sh. The potentially awkward pronunciation is corrected by adding an -es to those words. Here are a few examples.

tax + es = taxes

watch + es = watches

guess + es = guesses

mash + es = mashes

WORDS THAT END IN -o

There are two rules for words that end in -o, and—as usual—some exceptions. First, if the ending is a vowel followed by an *o*, simply add -s. Thus *cameo*, *duo*, and *rodeo* become *cameos*, *duos*, and *rodeos*. Second, if the word ends in a consonant followed by an *o*, add -es. Thus, *tornado*, *torpedo*, and *potato* become *tornadoes*, *torpedoes*, and *potatoes*.

There are a few exceptions to the rule for making plural forms of words that end in -o. The following words end in a consonant followed by an *o* but take only an -s:

albino–albinos

alto–altos

armadillo–armadillos

banjo–banjos

bronco–broncos

logo–logos

memo–memos

piano–pianos

silo–silos

solo–solos

soprano–sopranos

steno–stenos

WORDS THAT END IN -*y*

Words that end in -*y* are covered in greater detail in Lesson 22. Briefly, these words are made plural by adding -*s* when the word ends in a vowel + *y*, and changing the *y* to an *i* and adding -*es* when the word ends in a consonant + *y*. Examples include:

tray + s = trays

day + s = days

penny + es = pennies

candy + es = candies

WORDS THAT END IN -*f* OR -*fe*

Most words that end in -*f* or -*fe* require a letter change. Change the *f* or *fe* to *v* and then add -*es*. For example:

knife + es = knives

life + es = lives

elf + es = elves

wife + es = wives

There are a few exceptions to this rule that you will need to look out for. The exceptions include words that end in a double *f*, such as *sheriff*, *cuff*, and *plaintiff*. For these words, you only need to add an -*s* to the end to make them plural: *sheriffs*, *cuffs*, and *plaintiffs*. Other exceptions that you will need to memorize include *belief*, *chef*, *chief*, *gulf*, *roof*, and *safe*. All of those words retain their *f* and only require an -*s* to be added to the end: *beliefs*, *chefs*, *chiefs*, *gulfs*, *roofs*, and *safes*.

TIP: Hyphenated words are easier to pluralize than you might think. To make a hyphenated word plural, just add an -s to the word that is being pluralized. For example, if you are referring to more than one sister-in-law, you would write *sisters-in-law*, not *sister-in-laws*. Other examples include:

> fathers-in-law
> mothers-in-law
> ex-husbands
> ex-wives
> sergeants-at-arms

PRACTICE

Write the plural form of the following words.

1. tomato

2. lunch

3. wolf

4. ankle

5. pantry

6. sweater

7. earmuff

8. rich

9. thief

10. daughter-in-law

11. rash

12. navy

13. politician

14. buffalo

15. umbrella

ANSWERS

1. tomatoes
2. lunches
3. wolves
4. ankles
5. pantries
6. sweaters
7. earmuffs
8. riches
9. thieves
10. daughters-in-law
11. rashes
12. navies
13. politicians
14. buffaloes
15. umbrellas

irregular plurals

We dissect nature along lines laid down by our native language.
Language is not simply a reporting device for
experience but a defining framework for it.
—BENJAMIN LEE WHORF (1897–1941)
AMERICAN LINGUIST

Some words cannot be made plural by adding *-s* or *-es* to the end. This lesson will introduce you to irregular plurals and show you some tips to help you remember them.

AS YOU WILL HAVE noticed by now, the English language is filled with exceptions to the rules. Plurals are no different. A number of words do not follow the rules outlined in Lesson 20 for pluralizing words. Such words are considered irregular plurals.

Many of the words with irregular plurals have come into the English language from Latin or Greek. Because of this, you can find some patterns that will help you to remember how to pluralize these words. However, since the rules are not as straightforward as for regular plurals, you will need to spend some time memorizing the irregular plurals.

Here are several of the plurals that don't follow the *-es* and *-s* rules, grouped according to the patterns in the way their plurals are formed.

Words That End in *-um* or *-on*, Change to *-a*

curriculum	→ curricula	stratum	→	strata
datum	→ data	criterion	→	criteria
medium	→ media	phenomenon	→	phenomena

Words That End in *-is*, Change to *-es*

analysis	→ analyses	oasis	→	oases
axis	→ axes	parenthesis	→	parentheses
basis	→ bases	thesis	→	theses
hypothesis	→ hypotheses			

Words That End in *-us*, Change to *-i*

alumnus	→ alumni	nucleus	→	nuclei
focus	→ foci	thesaurus	→	thesauri
locus	→ loci			

Words That End in *-ex* or *-ix*, Change to *-ices*

appendix	→ appendices	index	→	indices
apex	→ apices	matrix	→	matrices

Words That End in *-eau*, Add an *-x*

beau	→ beaux	tableau	→	tableaux

Words That Require an Addition of or Change to *-en*

child	→ children	ox	→	oxen
man	→ men	woman	→	women

> **TIP:** Note that although the plural of *man* is *men* and the plural of *woman* is *women*, the plural of *human* is *humans*—not *humen*! Take care not to group the word *human* together with *man* and *woman* as far as forming the plural is concerned.

In addition to the irregular plurals that can be nicely grouped according to their patterns, there are some words that you will simply have to memorize because their plurals don't seem to make much sense. Here is a list of the most common of those irregular plurals.

alga	→	algae	nebula	→	nebulae
apparatus	→	apparatuses	person	→	people
die	→	dice	that	→	those
foot	→	feet	tooth	→	teeth
genus	→	genera	this	→	these
goose	→	geese	vertebra	→	vertebrae
louse	→	lice	vita	→	vitae
mouse	→	mice			

Some words can be pluralized in two different ways. These include:

Singular	Plural
antenna	antennae, antennas
appendix	appendices, appendixes
buffalo	buffalos, buffaloes
cactus	cacti, cactuses
dwarf	dwarfs, dwarves
fungus	fungi, funguses
hippopotamus	hippopotami, hippopotamuses
hoof	hoofs, hooves
index	indices, indexes
radius	radii, radiuses
syllabus	syllabi, syllabuses
symposium	symposia, symposiums
zero	zeros, zeroes

While there are some words that can be pluralized in different ways, there are also some words where you don't need to do anything to make them plural: the plural form of many animal names, and a few other words, is the same as the singular form. These words include:

> bison
>
> deer
>
> fish
>
> moose
>
> series
>
> sheep
>
> species

While you might be tempted to report that you came across several *meese* in your travels, you would correctly report that you saw several *moose*!

PRACTICE

Write the plural form of the following words.

1. ellipsis

2. bacterium

3. woman

4. alumnus

5. ovum

6. index

7. vertebra

8. deer

9. buffalo

10. hoof

11. oasis

12. goose

13. phenomenon

14. paralysis

15. matrix

ANSWERS

1. ellipses
2. bacteria
3. women
4. alumni
5. ova
6. indices *or* indexes
7. vertebrae
8. deer
9. buffaloes *or* buffalos
10. hoofs *or* hooves
11. oases
12. geese
13. phenomena
14. paralyses
15. matrices *or* matrixes

final *y*

Change your language and change your thoughts.
—KARL ALBRECHT (1920–)
GERMAN ENTREPRENEUR

This lesson covers how to add suffixes to words that end in -*y*.

IN LESSON 7, you learned about the rules for adding suffixes to words. While the concept of changing a final *y* to an *i* was introduced, it was not covered in depth. We'll do so in this lesson, where you'll learn which situations require you to change a final *y* to an *i* and which situations do not. In general, the rules that apply to the final *y* are fairly easy and consistent.

The rules for adding endings to words that end in *y* are:

- If the final *y* follows a consonant, change it to an *i* when adding any ending except -*ing*

  fly + *er* = *flier*, *fly* + *ing* = *flying*

- If the final *y* follows a vowel, it does not change, regardless of the ending

  toy + *ed* = *toyed*, *toy* + *ing* = *toying*

These rules apply to all endings, with the sole exception of -*ing*. With the -*ing* ending you always keep the final *y*. Let's take a look at some examples.

Change the *y* to *i* when adding *-ed*

party = partied	worry = worried
weary = wearied	try = tried

Change the *y* to *i* when adding *-er*

early = earlier	pretty = prettier
fly = flier	hungry = hungrier
sorry = sorrier	

Change the *y* to *i* when adding *-es*

party = parties	try = tries
marry = marries	fly = flies

Change the *y* to *i* when adding *-ness*

pretty = prettiness	silly = silliness
hearty = heartiness	crazy = craziness

Remember to keep the final *y* when adding *-ing*

fly = flying	worry = worrying
party = partying	try = trying
weary = wearying	marry = marrying

When the final *y* is preceded by a vowel, do not change it to *i*

enjoy = enjoyed, enjoying, enjoys	pray = prayed, praying, prays
employ = employed, employing, employs	delay = delayed, delaying, delays

PRACTICE

Complete the words below by deciding when to change the final *y* to *i*.

1. holy + ness =

2. study + ing =

3. comply + s =

4. sully + ed =

5. carry + ing =

6. destroy + ed =

7. say + ing =

8. drowsy + ness =

9. funny + er =

10. queasy + ness =

11. likely + er =

12. decay + s =

13. tidy + er =

14. spy + ing =

15. catchy + ness =

ANSWERS

1. holiness
2. studying
3. complies
4. sullied
5. carrying
6. destroyed
7. saying
8. drowsiness
9. funnier
10. queasiness
11. likelier
12. decays
13. tidier
14. spying
15. catchiness

LESSON 23

final *e*

*Language is the blood of the soul into which
thoughts run and out of which they grow.*
—OLIVER WENDELL HOLMES, SR. (1809–1894)
AMERICAN POET AND PHYSICIAN

This lesson focuses on the specific instances when you should drop the final *e* and when you should keep it when adding a suffix.

AS YOU PROBABLY have gathered by now, there are some words that require you to drop the final *e* and some that require you to keep it when adding a suffix. The basic rule of thumb is that you drop the final *e* when adding an ending that begins with a vowel, and you keep the final *e* when adding an ending that begins with a consonant.

Here are the rules to remember:

1. If the suffix begins with a vowel, drop the *e* when adding the suffix.
   type + -ist = typist
   drive + -able = drivable
   fortune + -ate = fortunate
2. If the suffix begins with a consonant, keep the final *e*.
   wise + -ly = wisely
   peace + -ful = peaceful
   coarse + -ness = coarseness

Let's start with a simple example, the word *parade*. When you add *-ed* or *-ing* to *parade*, you must first drop the final *e* to make *paraded* and *parading*. The combination of the word and those two endings is fairly straightforward and unlikely to cause you many problems. Since both endings begin with a vowel, you drop the final *e* before adding either of them to the word. To create the plural form, however, you keep the final *e*, making the word *parades*, because the plural ending, *s*, is a consonant.

Another example is the word *argue* and the endings *-ed*, *-ing*, *-able* , and *-s*. As in our preceding example, the first two endings are straightforward: you drop the final *e* to make *argued* and *arguing*. The third ending, *-able*, is a little trickier. Many times, people will keep the final *e*, even though the ending begins with a vowel, writing *argueable* when the correct spelling is *arguable*. Remember to drop the final *e* when an ending begins with a vowel and to keep the final *e* when the ending begins with a consonant (*s*), to make the word *argues*.

As with most spelling rules, there are exceptions pertaining to the final *e*. There are two situations when you *keep* the final *e* when adding an ending that begins with a vowel. Both of these exceptions make sense when you keep punctuation in mind.

1. Keep the final *e* when it follows a soft *c* or *g*, in order to maintain the soft sound of those letters. If you look back at Lesson 14, you will recall that when *c* or *g* are followed by *a*, *o*, or *u*, the consonant makes a hard sound. To keep the soft sound, you must keep the final *e* in words such as *courage* (+ *-ous* = *courageous*), *outrage* (+ *-ous* = *outrageous*), and *notice* (+*-able* = *noticeable*). Other words, such as *binge* (+ = *-ing* = *bingeing*) seem to ignore the rule entirely: *g* followed by *i* would normally have a soft sound in any case.
2. Also keep the final *e* to show that a preceding vowel should be long. For example, *hoe* + *-ing* = *hoeing* (not *hoing*). Again, the final *e* is kept to preserve the correct pronunciation of the word.

A silent *e* at the end of a word is always dropped when adding a suffix that begins with a consonant. Some common examples are:

acknowledge + *-ment* = *acknowledgment*

argue + *-ment* = *argument*

awe + *-ful* = *awful*

due + *-ly* = *duly*

judge + *-ment* = *judgment*

nine + -th = ninth
true + -ly = truly
whole + -ly = wholly
wise + -dom = wisdom

PRACTICE

Choose the correctly spelled word in each of the following sentences.

1. Andy's mother prided herself on being an excellent *typist / typeist*.

2. They told the salesperson they were only *browseing / browsing*.

3. Jenny *encourageed / encouraged* her sister to go to college.

4. They were *baking / bakeing* cookies for the bake sale.

5. They didn't notice that the flames were *singing / singeing* the stockings hung on the mantel.

6. Emily took advantage of every *opportunity / opportuneity* she was offered.

7. That was a *surpriseing / surprising* turn of events!

8. Her voice had a certain *hoarsness / hoarseness* that others found annoying.

9. All of the dancers were quite *graceful / gracful*.

10. The call was not *traceable / tracable*.

11. Jackson wished the others wouldn't be so *judgemental / judgmental*.

12. They went straight to accounts *receivable / receiveable*.

13. Hannah had a lot of *valuable / valueable* jewelry.

14. Steve wasn't very good at *gaugeing / gauging* worth.

15. They were *desperately / desperatly* looking for answers.

ANSWERS

1. Andy's mother prided herself on being an excellent *typist*.

2. They told the salesperson they were only *browsing*.

3. Jenny *encouraged* her sister to go to college.

4. They were *baking* cookies for the bake sale.

5. They didn't notice that the flames were *singeing* the stockings hung on the mantel.

6. Emily took advantage of every *opportunity* she was offered.

7. That was a *surprising* turn of events!

8. Her voice had a certain *hoarseness* that others found annoying.

9. All of the dancers were quite *graceful*.

10. The call was not *traceable*.

11. Jackson wished the others wouldn't be so *judgmental*.

12. They went straight to accounts *receivable*.

13. Hannah had a lot of *valuable* jewelry.

14. Steve wasn't very good at *gauging* worth.

15. They were *desperately* looking for answers.

doubling final consonants

Language is not an abstract construction of the learned, or of dictionary makers, but is something arising out of the work, needs, ties, joys, affections, tastes, of long generations of humanity, and has its basis broad and low, close to the ground.
—Noah Webster (1758–1843)
American lexicographer

This lesson will cover the last of the special situations where a word must undergo changes before an ending can be added to it.

AS YOU ARE no doubt beginning to realize, there are many rules that govern the changes that words require when suffixes are added to them. There are rules that tell you which types of suffixes can be added to which types of words. Then there are rules about words that end in *y* and *e*. Now, we'll learn about words that require you to double their final consonants when adding an ending.

At first glance, you may see no logical reason why final consonants are sometimes doubled and sometimes not. But in fact, there are three simple yet key rules that govern the doubling of consonants before a suffix. When adding a suffix to a word that ends in a consonant, you double that consonant if

- the ending begins with a vowel: *run + ing = running, log + ed = logged*
- the last syllable of the word is accented and that syllable ends in a single consonant preceded by a single vowel: *begin + ing = beginning*

(words of only one syllable are accented by definition and therefore follow the same rule: *stop + er = stopper*)

You might want to refer back to Lesson 7 for a list of common suffixes, and pick
out those that begin with vowels.

....

TIP: Many people have trouble with the word *occur*. But you can master its spelling by remembering the consonant-doubling rules you have
just learned. *Occur* becomes *occurring*, *occurred*, and *occurrence*. The final
consonant in *occur* is doubled because the last syllable in the word is
accented and that syllable ends in a single consonant preceded by a single vowel. The word *occur* already contains a double consonant pair—
cc—so people may be reluctant to double the final *r*. Don't be afraid to
have two sets of double consonants in a word if it fits the requirements
for doubling the final consonant.

....

Here are some examples of words that meet the doubling requirements for
final consonants when you add an ending that begins with a vowel.

run = running, runner, runny

slam = slammed, slamming, slammer

nag = nagged, nagging

incur = incurred, incurring

kid = kidded, kidding, kidder

plan = planned, planning, planner

begin = beginning, beginner

set = setting, setter

transmit = transmitted, transmitting, transmittal

beg = begged, begging, beggar

submit = submitted, submitting, submittal, submitter

grin = grinned, grinning, grinner

When adding a suffix that begins with a vowel to a word that ends in a consonant, you do *not* double that consonant if

- the accent is on the first syllable: *cover + ed = covered*
- the final consonant is preceded by another consonant rather than by a single vowel: *part + ing = parting*
- the final consonant is preceded by more than one vowel: *sleep + er = sleeper*

....

TIP: There are a few exceptions to the rules for doubling final consonants. Some words that seem to fit the requirements actually don't double the final consonant. Two exceptions are

bus + es = buses and *chagrin + ed = chagrined*

In addition, most words that end in *-w* or *-x* do not double their final consonant:

draw = drawer, drawing
few = fewer
show = showing, shower, showed
glow = glowed, glowing, glower
tax = taxed, taxing, taxable
wax = waxed, waxing

....

PRACTICE

Mark the words *yes* or *no* with a checkmark depending on whether or not they meet the requirements for doubling the final consonant before adding an ending that begins with a vowel.

	Yes	No
1. meet	_____	_____
2. mop	_____	_____
3. look	_____	_____

	Yes	No
4. seal	___	___
5. drink	___	___
6. bet	___	___
7. discover	___	___
8. clap	___	___
9. pump	___	___
10. walk	___	___
11. tip	___	___
12. ramp	___	___
13. think	___	___
14. eat	___	___
15. stop	___	___
16. jump	___	___
17. shovel	___	___
18. relax	___	___
19. read	___	___
20. ram	___	___

ANSWERS

	Yes	No
1. meet		✔ (consonant is preceded by two vowels)
2. mop	✔	
3. look		✔ (consonant is preceded by two vowels)
4. seal		✔ (consonant is preceded by two vowels)
5. drink		✔ (consonant is preceded by another consonant)
6. bet	✔	
7. discover		✔ (accent is not on last syllable)
8. clap	✔	
9. pump		✔ (consonant is preceded by another consonant)
10. walk		✔ (consonant is preceded by another consonant)
11. tip	✔	
12. ramp		✔ (consonant is preceded by another consonant)
13. think		✔ (consonant is preceded by another consonant)
14. eat		✔ (consonant is preceded by two vowels)
15. stop	✔	
16. jump		✔ (consonant is preceded by another consonant)
17. shovel		✔ (accent is not on last syllable)
18. relax		✔ (ends in x)
19. read		✔ (consonant is preceded by two vowels)
20. ram	✔	

S E C T I O N 5

special situations

JUST AS SPELLING RULES are filled with exceptions, the English language is filled with confusing and tricky words. There are words that sound alike but are spelled differently, words that are spelled alike but sound differently, and words that are so frequently spelled or used incorrectly that their correct spelling and usage may even seem foreign to you. Then there are actual foreign words, for which the general rules you have learned do not apply, and there are business, legal, technological, and literary terms that can make your head spin. Don't worry: this final section will clarify all of these special situations.

homonyms

Life is tons of discipline. Your first discipline is your vocabulary;
then your grammar and your punctuation. Then, in your
exuberance and bounding energy you say you're going to
add to that. Then you add rhyme and meter.
And your delight is in that power.
—ROBERT FROST (1874–1963)
AMERICAN POET

The English language is filled with words that sound alike but are spelled differently, and words that are spelled alike but pronounced differently. In both cases, the words have different meanings. This lesson will set you straight on such words.

HOMONYM. HOMOPHONE. HOMOGRAPH. These terms can be confusing. They sound and look so similar that you may wonder whether they all mean the same thing. The short answer is not exactly, but they are related. The words that fall into each category are often the root of spelling mishaps.

Before we get into how to avoid those mishaps, let's take a look at the three terms, what they mean, and how they relate. *Homonyms* are pairs (of even larger groups) of words that have different meanings but either are pronounced alike but spelled differently or are spelled alike but pronounced differently.

The first type of homonym, words with the same pronunciation but different spellings, are called *homophones*. Examples of homophones include *deer* and *dear*, *allowed* and *aloud*, and *bare* and *bear*.

The second type of homonyms, words with the same spelling but (usually) different pronunciation are called *homographs*. Examples of homographs include *present* (with the accent on the first syllable, meaning *gift*) and *present* (accent on the second syllable, meaning *to introduce*) and *conduct* (with the accent on the first syllable, meaning *behavior*) and *conduct* (accent on the second syllable, meaning *to lead*). Homographs that are pronounced alike include, for example, *saw* (which is both the past tense of *see* and an implement for cutting wood) and *part* (which can mean a portion of a whole or to leave each other).

Now that you know what homonyms, homophones, and homographs are, you're ready to learn how to avoid misusing them. In general, most errors with homonyms come from carelessness. By paying attention to the words you use and what they mean, as well as by carefully proofreading your work, you can avoid most errors. Frequently made errors can become habits; you can avoid them by learning the proper usage of homonym pairs.

....

TIP: As you become more familiar with homonyms, pay special attention to how you use them. If you are writing a sentence containing the word *their*, for example, take a moment to make sure that you don't mean *there*. Pausing to think about the meaning of the word you are using will help you choose the correct one!

....

COMMON HOMONYMS

We could fill an entire book just with the homonym pairs that exist in the English language. For the purpose of this book, though, we'll look at the most common homonyms; the ones that you are most likely to use in your day-to-day life.

The following list includes some common homonym pairs and a very brief definition or explanation of each word. The list is divided into homophones and homographs.

Homophone Pair	Definition
ad	short for *advertisement*
add	to calculate the total
allowed	permitted
aloud	spoken

Homophone Pair	Definition
bare	to show
bear	to withstand
beat	to hit
beet	root vegetable
board	a piece of wood
bored	uninterested
bough	tree branch
bow	to bend at the waist
brake	device that stops a vehicle
break	to split apart
by	near or beside
buy	to acquire something by payment
capital	seat of government
capitol	government building
cell	small room, as in a jail
sell	to trade for money
cent	coin (one-hundredth of a dollar)
sent	past tense of *send*
cite	to refer to
sight	vision
site	location
coarse	rough
course	path
complement	to complete
compliment	to praise
council	group of leaders
counsel	attorney, advisor
dear	beloved
deer	forest animal with antlers
die	to cease living
dye	substance that creates color
dual	double
duel	fight between two people, using weapons
fair	considering all sides
fare	payment for travel or admission

Homophone Pair	Definition
feat	accomplishment
feet	certain body parts
find	locate
fined	to pay a penalty (past tense)
flour	baking ingredient
flower	plant
foreword	introduction to a book
forward	toward the front
gait	the way one walks or runs
gate	a door in a fence
grate	to shred
great	excellent
heal	to cure
heel	the back of the foot
hear	to listen to
here	in this place
knew	past tense of *know*
new	having just come to be
loan	something lent
lone	single
overdo	to do too much
overdue	late payment
pain	ache
pane	panel of glass
pair	two
pear	fruit
passed	moved beyond
past	time before the present
peace	opposite of war
piece	small part of
peal	ring
peel	outer shell of fruit
pedal	device operated by the foot
peddle	to sell
peer	equal
pier	landing place for ships

Homophone Pair	Definition
plain	humble
plane	flying machine
principal	person in charge
principle	standard
rain	state of weather
reign	to rule
rein	rope used for steering a horse
right	correct
rite	ritual
wright	one who makes something
write	to compose, as language
scene	part of a play
seen	past participle of *see*
soar	fly
sore	painful
stationary	not moving
stationery	writing paper
tail	hindmost appendage on an animal
tale	story
team	group working together
teem	filled with
their	belonging to them
there	that place
they're	contraction of *they are*
vain	having a large ego
vein	blood vessel
vary	to change
very	extremely
waist	area of the body above the hips
waste	to misuse
weak	not strong
week	seven-day period
weather	state of atmosphere
whether	conjunction that introduces alternatives

Homophone Pair	Definition
which	what one?
witch	person with magic powers
who's	contraction of *who is*
whose	belonging to someone

Homograph	Brief Definitions
address	1. directions for delivery 2. place of residence
bass	1. type of fish 2. stringed instrument
bow	1. to bend at the waist 2. flexible wood used for shooting arrows
close	1. to be near 2. to shut
conflict	1. to disagree 2. disagreement
desert	1. to leave 2. an arid, barren place
does	1. a questioning verb 2. more than one female deer
dove	1. a white bird 2. past tense of *dive*
lead	1. at the front position 2. substance used in pencils
live	1. to reside 2. not prerecorded
minute	1. one-sixtieth of an hour 2. very small
produce	1. to create, to generate 2. fruits and vegetables
read	1. to examine and understand the meanings of written words 2. past tense of *read*

Homograph	Brief Definitions
record	1. to write or document something
	2. list of achievements
separate	1. disconnected
	2. to keep apart
tear	1. a watery fluid released from the eyes
	2. to rip
well	1. an interjection used to introduce a thought
	2. to be in satisfactory health
wind	1. to wrap around or coil
	2. air velocity or movement
wound	1. wrapped around
	2. injury

PRACTICE

Choose the correct italicized word to complete each sentence.

1. The new shopping mall is being built on this *site / cite*.

2. It isn't always easy to *adapt / adopt* to life's big changes.

3. The bag *compliments / complements* that outfit nicely.

4. The weather is supposed to be *fair / fare* and sunny this weekend.

5. Brandon was selling candy bars to raise money for his baseball *team / teem*.

6. We weren't allowed to take any *access / excess* baggage on the flight.

7. Henry had the *write / right* answers to all the multiple choice questions.

8. I bought monogrammed *stationary / stationery* to send my thank-you notes.

9. Alice planned to *great / grate* cheese for the pizza.

10. I liked to watch the birds *soar / sore* through the sky.

ANSWERS

1. The new shopping mall is being built on this *site*.
2. It isn't always easy to *adapt* to life's big changes.
3. The bag *complements* that outfit nicely.
4. The weather is supposed to be *fair* and sunny this weekend.
5. Brandon was selling candy bars to raise money for his baseball *team*.
6. We weren't allowed to take any *excess* baggage on the flight.
7. Henry had the *right* answers to all the multiple choice questions.
8. I bought monogrammed *stationery* to send my thank-you notes.
9. Alice planned to *grate* cheese for the pizza.
10. I liked to watch the birds *soar* through the sky.

frequently misspelled words

If a word in the dictionary were misspelled, how would we know?
—STEVEN WRIGHT (1955–)
AMERICAN COMEDIAN

Certain words are frequently misspelled by even the best spellers. In this lesson, you'll see why some of these words are misspelled, and review a list of the most commonly misspelled words.

PEOPLE MISSPELL WORDS for a host of reasons. Many of the most commonly misspelled words, however, have one of four characteristics in common. These characteristics are double-letter combination, confusion between *c* and *s*, misuse of *-able* / *-ible*, and misuse of *-ance* and *-ence*.

1. **Double-letter combination.** Many words with double letters are misspelled with single letters. For instance, the words *accommodate*, *possess*, *committee*, *occurrence*, and *millennium* often have their double letters erroneously written as single letters. Other times, double-letter combinations are used where they shouldn't be. The word *harass* is often written as *harrass*, for example, and *fulfill* as *fullfill*.

2. **Confusion between *c* and *s*.** When *c* and *s* both appear in the same word, they often cause confusion, leading people to use the wrong letter. The words *absence*, *descend*, *license*, and *discipline* are often

misspelled. If you have trouble with words that contain both *c* and *s*, you might want to create a mnemonic for those words.

3. **Misuse of *-able / -ible*.** Since these suffixes are pronounced alike, it can be difficult to remember which words are spelled with *-able* and which with *-ible*. Keep in mind that *-able* is most often added to words that can stand alone such as *regrettable*, *manageable*, or *noticeable*. The suffix *-ible*, on the other hand, is added to roots that cannot stand alone, such as *eligible* or *susceptible*.

4. **Misuse of *-ance / -ence*.** Here again, you can't rely on pronunciation to tell you whether to use *-ance* or *-ence*. What you can do is determine which words ending in *-ance* or *-ence* you have trouble with, and then exaggerate the *a* or *e* sound in the endings. For example, you would stress the *a* in *-ance* in the words *resemblance*, *abundance*, *maintenance*, and *acquaintance*, and the *e* in *-ence* in the words *independence*, *persistence*, *coincidence*, and *correspondence*.

COMMONLY MISSPELLED WORDS

The following list contains 150 commonly misspelled words; they are all spelled correctly in the list. As you read through this list, be alert to those words whose spelling surprises you. Pay special attention to these words and add them to your master list of words that you need to practice and learn.

One way to use this list effectively is to read through it and check off the words that you thought were spelled differently. Then, go back through the checked words to see whether you can find any patterns. Do you have a hard time with certain vowel combinations? Are there particular suffixes that give you trouble? If you notice any patterns that emerge, spend some extra time on the lessons that apply to them.

absence	alleged	bulletin
abundance	ambiguous	calendar
accidentally	analysis	canceled
accommodate	annual	cannot
acknowledgment	argument	cemetery
acquaintance	awkward	coincidence
aggravate	basically	collectible
alibi	boundary	committee

comparative	grievance	occasionally
completely	guarantee	occurred
condemn	guidance	omission
congratulations	harass	opportunity
conscientious	hindrance	outrageous
consistent	ideally	pamphlet
convenient	implement	parallel
correspondence	independence	perceive
deceive	indispensable	permanent
definitely	inoculate	perseverance
dependent	insufficient	personnel
depot	interference	possess
descend	interrupt	potato
desperate	jealousy	precede
development	jewelry	preferred
dilemma	judgment	prejudice
discrepancy	leisure	prevalent
eighth	liaison	privilege
eligible	length	procedure
embarrass	lenient	proceed
equivalent	lieutenant	prominent
euphoria	lightning	pronunciation
existence	loophole	quandary
exuberance	losing	questionnaire
feasible	maintenance	receipt
February	maneuver	receive
fifth	mathematics	recommend
forcibly	millennium	reference
forfeit	minuscule	referred
formerly	miscellaneous	regardless
fourth	misspell	relevant
fulfill	negotiable	religious
grateful	ninth	remembrance

reservoir	separate	ubiquitous
responsible	souvenir	unanimous
restaurant	specifically	usually
rhythm	sufficient	usurp
ridiculous	supersede	vacuum
roommate	temperament	vengeance
scary	temperature	visible
scissors	truly	Wednesday
secretary	twelfth	wherever

PRACTICE

Unscramble the letters to create correctly spelled words from the list in this lesson.

1. I I B L V S E

2. R A D E P S E T E

3. T H R F O U

4. R E V C E E I

5. T A R S Y E R C E

6. H R Y H T M

7. R P O E C E D

8. B A S C E E N

9. L R Y J E E W

10. A M C M O D A C O T E

11. L I S A O N I

12. L L P A L A R E

13. O R M F E R Y L

14. U G N A E T E R A

15. N O I U C T E L A

ANSWERS

1. visible
2. desperate
3. fourth
4. receive
5. secretary
6. rhythm
7. proceed
8. absence
9. jewelry
10. accommodate
11. liaison
12. parallel
13. formerly
14. guarantee
15. inoculate

commonly confused words

*Nature is a temple in which living columns sometimes emit
confused words. Man approaches it through forests of
symbols, which observe him with familiar glances.*
—CHARLES BAUDELAIRE (1821–1867)
FRENCH POET

There are hundreds of word pairs that either sound similar, are spelled similarly, or have similar meanings, causing them to be confused or misused. This lesson outlines the most commonly confused words and provides you with tips for using the correct words in your writing.

THERE ARE MANY commonly confused words which, although they are not homonyms, have similarities that cause them to be mistaken for one another. Many of these confusing words sound similar but are quite different in meaning. The words *accept* and *except*, for example, which sound almost alike, mean entirely different things and are not at all interchangeable. *Accept* means to recognize or to receive willingly; *except* means to exclude. As you can see, the words have two very different meanings. So, if you use *accept* when you mean *except*, you are not conveying your message accurately.

Some words are confusing because different prefixes give them different meanings. For example, *disinterested* and *uninterested* (defined in the list that follows), mean two very different things.

In fact, your writing suffers whenever you misuse words. If you use words incorrectly on a college application, for example, you could ruin your chances of being accepted.

In order to ensure that you are using the correct word, you must know its meaning. The importance of word meanings was covered in Lesson 4. The tips included in that lesson are relevant to this lesson, so be sure that you understand the material covered there before moving on.

....

TIP: Pay attention to the meaning of every word you use in your writing and in your speaking. If you are unsure whether or not the word you are using is correct, look it up in the dictionary or refer to the list of commonly confused words in this lesson.

....

LIST OF COMMONLY CONFUSED WORDS

The following list contains some of the most commonly confused word pairs, along with a very brief definition of each word. As you read through the list, make note of any words that you misuse frequently.

Word Pair	Brief Definition
accept	to recognize, to receive willingly
except	excluding, but, with the exception of
access	means of approaching
excess	extra
adapt	to adjust
adopt	to take as one's own
affect	to influence, to pretend
effect	result, to make happen
affluent	wealthy
effluent	flowing out
all ready	completely prepared
already	previously
allusion	indirect reference to something
illusion	fantasy that may be confused with reality

Word Pair	Brief Definition
among	in the middle of several
between	in an interval separating two
assure	to make someone feel confident
ensure	to make certain
insure	to guarantee against loss or harm
beside	at the side of
besides	in addition to
continual	constantly
continuous	uninterrupted
decent	well mannered
descent	decline, fall
device	apparatus or machinery
devise	to develop or create an idea, system, or product
disinterested	no strong opinion either way
uninterested	having no interest in
elicit	to draw out
illicit	illegal
eminent	well-known
imminent	pending
explicit	openly or fully expressed
implicit	hinted at indirectly
farther	at or to a greater distance, beyond
further	to advance, additional
imply	to hint, to suggest
infer	to assume, to deduce
lay	to set down, to place something (also past tense of *lie*, meaning to recline)
lie	to recline (*also* to tell a falsehood)
loose	not tight
lose	unable to find
may be	is a possibility
maybe	perhaps
persecute	to mistreat
prosecute	to take legal action

Word Pair	Brief Definition
personal	individual
personnel	employees
precede	to go before
proceed	to continue
proceeds	profits
than	in contrast to
then	next in time
who	substitute for *he, she, they*
whom	substitute for *him, her, them*

PRACTICE

Unscramble the letters to find the words that match each definition.

1. not tight   OSOLE

2. to mistreat   SECPUTREE

3. to set down   YLA

4. illegal   CILTIIL

5. wealthy   FUELAFNT

6. extra   CSEXES

7. to make certain   SREENU

8. to hint, to suggest   PYILM

9. well-mannered   CDEETN

10. to adjust   AAPTD

ANSWERS

1. loose
2. persecute
3. lay
4. illicit
5. affluent
6. excess
7. ensure
8. imply
9. decent
10. adapt

business, legal, and technological terms

I prefer the honest jargon of reality to the outright lies of books.
—JEAN ROSTAND (1894–1977)
FRENCH WRITER, BIOLOGIST, AND PHILOSOPHER

This lesson covers a sampling of work-related terms and provides instruction on how to familiarize yourself with them.

YOU MAY BE a long way off from your first job, but that doesn't mean you can't pay attention to some of the terms that are used in the business world. Business, legal, and technological terms are to be found in newspapers and magazine articles as well as in the workplace. If you become familiar with them now, you will be at an advantage when you finally do enter the workforce.

Another benefit of learning work-related words is that they will help you to keep up on current events. If you read newspapers, magazines, or websites to learn about current events, chances are you will come across financial, legal, or other business terms. Understanding these terms will help you understand the message that the author is trying to convey. When you are called upon to write essays on current events or business-related issues, your spelling of these terms will be important.

You can improve your spelling of work-related terms by learning the words listed in this lesson and by reading business journals, magazines, books, and websites. Business books are especially helpful because they often include glossaries to augment their content. Business magazines and websites usually feature timely topics and use current terms, jargon, or buzzwords. Learning the proper spelling of these terms can be helpful to you as you further your education and when you eventually embark on a career.

INTERNET RESOURCES

Here is a list of some work-related websites that you can visit to familiarize yourself with business, legal, and technological terms. As you work your way through these sites, you will undoubtedly find links to others. Visit those sites as well, read their articles, and look at any resources or glossaries they offer.

Barron's Online: www.barrons.com

Bloomberg.com: www.bloomberg.com

Business Journals: www.bizjournals.com

New York Times **Online:** www.nytimes.com

The Wall Street Journal **Online:** www.wsj.com

Fast Company **Magazine Online:** www.fastcompany.com

Internet.com: www.internet.com

Women in Technology International: www.witi.org

CNN: www.cnn.com

WORK-RELATED TERMS

The following list is a small sample of work-related terms. Each of the 50 words in the list is accompanied by a brief definition. If you follow the suggestions outlined in this lesson, you will begin to notice these terms in the material that you read. Use this guide and your dictionary to increase your knowledge of work-related terms.

1. acquisition: something that is acquired or gained
2. adjudicate: to make a judicial decision
3. application: a software program that lets you complete a task on your computer, such as word processing, listening to music, or viewing a web page

4. balance: the difference between money available and money owed

5. bandwidth: the capacity for sending information through an Internet connection

6. bankrupt: the legal state of being unable to pay one's debts

7. benefits: anything offered by an employer in addition to salary, including health insurance, vacation days, and sick days

8. blogosphere: a collective term for the community of blogs and bloggers

9. branding: a marketing term for the definition of a company for advertising purposes

10. browser: the program that enables users to look at files on the Web

11. commercial: relating to commerce, the exchange of goods; items offered for sale

12. compatible: able to work together; often used to describe software or computer devices

13. consortium: an association of two or more individuals or companies operating collectively

14. consumer: individual who uses goods or services

15. content: substantive information

16. corporation: a company that is legally treated as an individual

17. credit: money due to a person or a business

18. database: an organizational system using tables that helps a computer quickly retrieve pieces of information

19. debt: money owed by a person or a business

20. department: a smaller division within a company

21. deposition: witness testimony given under oath during the trial preparation process

22. digital: description of any electronic device that uses numbers to calculate information

23. diversity: a state consisting of a variety of different elements; often used in reference to economic matters

24. employer: business or individual for whom an employee works

25. equity: ownership

26. exempt: not subject to rules; often used in reference to workers and Fair Labor Standards Act regulations

27. fiscal: financial

28. globalization: the state of extending to all parts of the globe; often used in reference to economic matters

29. implement: to put into effect

30. incur: to come into or to acquire, usually undesirably
31. insurance: a coverage plan in which an individual pays a regular fee in exchange for future services
32. interview: a formal meeting set up between an employer and a potential employee seeking to be hired for a job
33. jargon: the specialized vocabulary of an industry or group
34. liability: a financial obligation such as a debt
35. litigious: inclined to engage in lawsuits
36. multimedia: media and content that use a combination of different forms
37. network: a group of two or more computers linked together
38. outsource: to contract jobs to outside workers
39. policy: a course of action; a rule
40. procedure: a way of doing something
41. product: a thing being created or manufactured
42. references: a group of people presented by a potential employee to an employer who can report on the potential employee's strengths and weaknesses
43. resume: a printed overview of an employee's, or potential employee's, previous job and educational experience
44. revenue: the amount of money that an individual or company receives during a set period of time
45. salary: the amount of money that a job pays, usually figured as an annual amount
46. spreadsheet: a bookkeeping program that displays data in rows and columns, or any individual document created by such a program
47. sustainable: capable of being continued with minimal long-term environmental effects
48. transparent: open about operating procedures
49. upload: to copy to an outside source from a computer or network location
50. virtual: carried on through a computer

PRACTICE

The following list of terms includes words from this lesson as well as work-related terms that were not covered here. Some of the terms are spelled correctly and some are not. For each term, mark whether the spelling is correct or incorrect. If you don't know what a word in the list means, take this opportunity to look it up in the dictionary.

	Correct	Incorrect
1. forcast	_____	_____
2. harass	_____	_____
3. consumer	_____	_____
4. arbitage	_____	_____
5. benificiary	_____	_____
6. revenew	_____	_____
7. fiscall	_____	_____
8. exemt	_____	_____
9. acquisition	_____	_____
10. collussion	_____	_____
11. equaty	_____	_____
12. subsidy	_____	_____
13. financial	_____	_____
14. comerrcial	_____	_____

	Correct	Incorrect
15. nepotism	_____	_____
16. impliment	_____	_____
17. salary	_____	_____
18. bankrupt	_____	_____
19. aplication	_____	_____
20. globalization	_____	_____

ANSWERS

1. incorrect—forecast
2. correct
3. correct
4. incorrect—arbitrage
5. incorrect—beneficiary
6. incorrect—revenue
7. incorrect—fiscal
8. incorrect—exempt
9. correct
10. incorrect—collusion
11. incorrect—equity
12. correct
13. correct
14. incorrect—commercial
15. correct
16. incorrect—implement
17. correct
18. correct
19. incorrect—application
20. correct

literary terms

*Language shapes the way we think, and
determines what we can think about.*
—BENJAMIN LEE WHORF (1897–1941)
AMERICAN LINGUIST

In this lesson, you'll learn why literary terms are important and how they are used outside of the classroom.

IN YOUR ENGLISH classes, you have probably encountered many literary terms such as *genre, metaphor, figurative language,* and *anthropomorphism.* Perhaps you learned the terms and promptly forgot them when you moved on to the next lesson; this is common, but unfortunate. All the terms you learned in your English classes have meanings beyond the realm of literature and language. Using such terms well—and spelling them correctly—will enhance your writing, allowing you to convey more nuanced meaning with every sentence.

Are you wondering how you could possibly use literary terms in your everyday life? Consider how frequently you read the word *irony* in articles and essays and on websites and blogs. This literary term is commonly used in areas that have little to do with literature. In fact, a recent Google search on the word returned more than 18.7 million hits! Being familiar with a common term such as *irony,* with its roots as a literary device, will greatly improve your ability to use the word correctly, and to understand it fully when someone else uses it.

Let's take a look at another example. An article in *The New York Times* during the 2008 presidential election described then-Senator Obama as *grounding his lofty* rhetoric *in the more prosaic language of white-working-class discontent*. Clearly, the article was not discussing literary theory or the merits of a particular short story but was simply using the literary term *rhetoric* to address a timely issue.

The selective and proper use of literary terms can enhance your writing. This will benefit you greatly as you write essays for school, craft personal statements for college applications, and deal with correspondence when you enter the working world.

You can easily expand your knowledge of literary terms by reading study guides for popular literary fiction, journals dedicated to literary theory, or anthologies that include study guides or lessons. Many of your English textbooks and anthologies have glossaries that can be wonderful resources for learning literary terms. Book reviews in your local newspaper or your favorite magazines will also yield some new words. And, of course, the Internet is full of websites geared toward literature, language, and critical theory.

INTERNET RESOURCES

Here is a list of websites that you can visit to familiarize yourself with literary terms. As you work your way through these sites, you will undoubtedly find links to others. Visit those sites as well, read their articles, and look at any resources or glossaries they offer.

> **Gale Glossary of Terms:** www.gale.cengage.com/free_resources/ glossary
>
> **Glossary of Literary Terms:** www.uncp.edu/home/canada/ work/allam/general/glossary.htm
>
> **Glossary of Rhetorical Terms:** www.uky.edu/AS/Classics/ rhetoric.html
>
> **Virtual Salt Glossary of Literary Terms:** www.virtualsalt.com/ litterms.htm
>
> **Wordwizard:** http://www.wordwizard.com

COMMON LITERARY TERMS

The following table includes 23 commonly used literary terms, their meanings, and some sticky spelling situations that you should watch out for. Use this list as a starting point for developing your own list of high-impact literary terms.

Literary Term	Meaning	Watch Out!
anecdote	a short account of an interesting or humorous incident	begins with *anec*, not *anic*
archetype	an original model or type after which other similar things are patterned	begins with *arche*, not *archa*
climax	the crucial moment in a story	ends with *x*
figurative	not literal	begins with *figura*, not *figure*
foreshadow	to hint at what will happen later	one word; not *forshadow*
hyperbole	intentional exaggeration	ends with *e*, not *y*
interpret	to explain the meaning of	ends with *pret*, not *pert*
irony	use of words to express something different from the literal meaning	spelled as it sounds
literal	actual meaning	ends with *al*, not *el*
oxymoron	figure of speech combining two contradictory terms	no hypen
personification	giving an inanimate object or animal humanlike properties	includes *nif*, not *naf*
plot	course of events in a story	spelled as it sounds
protagonist	main character in a story	begins with *pro*, not *pra*
pun	play on words	spelled as it sounds
rhetoric	style of speaking	don't forget the *h*
satire	literary style in which important topics are made to look ridiculous through the use of humor	only one *t*
setting	environment or location in which a story takes place	double *t*

Literary Term	Meaning	Watch Out!
simile	figure of speech that compares two unlike things	ends with *e*, not *y*
summarize	to highlight the most important details	double *m*
theme	main idea of a story	spelled as it sounds
tone	feeling of a story	spelled as it sounds
travesty	debased or inferior imitation	only one *v*
trite	worn out from overuse	spelled as it sounds

PRACTICE

Find these 15 literary terms in the puzzle: theme, irony, rhetoric, trite, climax, foreshadow, archetype, satire, travesty, literal, pun, setting, oxymoron, hyperbole, simile. (The words may appear vertically, horizontally, diagonally, backward, or forward.)

A	E	M	E	H	T	X	B	B	U	M	S	A	T	I
F	H	O	R	Y	L	L	R	H	E	T	O	R	I	C
J	K	R	H	N	X	K	X	P	U	R	R	L	C	K
L	O	P	E	O	R	A	C	T	R	I	T	E	F	N
F	L	I	T	R	M	H	Y	U	D	R	B	K	J	N
Y	O	A	L	I	T	E	R	A	L	G	H	B	U	J
T	E	R	L	S	A	T	Y	B	H	J	F	P	G	H
S	H	C	E	R	I	T	A	S	Y	V	J	F	O	O
E	D	H	D	S	D	B	J	M	X	W	S	W	X	Y
A	W	T	R	T	Y	A	U	N	M	C	T	D	M	X
R	A	Y	Z	C	E	R	D	G	H	R	T	L	O	I
T	C	P	L	I	T	W	V	O	N	T	I	F	R	O
S	R	E	F	O	R	D	T	G	W	B	N	V	O	R
S	I	M	I	L	E	C	C	M	L	E	G	R	N	T

ANSWERS

```
A  E  M  E  H  T  X  B  B  U  M  S  A  T  I
F  H  O  R  Y  L  L  R  H  E  T  O  R  I  C
J  K  R  H  N  X  K  X  P  U  R  R  L  C  K
L  O  P  E  O  R  A  C  T  R  I  T  E  F  N
F  L  I  T  R  M  H  Y  U  D  R  B  K  J  N
Y  O  A  L  I  T  E  R  A  L  G  H  B  U  J
T  E  R  L  S  A  T  Y  B  H  J  F  P  G  H
S  H  C  E  R  I  T  A  S  Y  V  J  F  O  O
E  D  H  D  S  D  B  J  M  X  W  S  W  X  Y
V  S  E  E  E  H  E  L  O  B  R  E  P  Y  H
A  W  T  R  T  Y  A  U  N  M  C  T  D  M  X
R  A  Y  Z  C  E  R  D  G  H  R  T  L  O  I
T  C  P  L  I  T  W  V  O  N  T  I  F  R  O
S  R  E  F  O  R  D  T  G  W  B  N  V  O  R
S  I  M  I  L  E  C  C  M  L  E  G  R  N  T
```

foreign words

*Those who know nothing of foreign languages
know nothing of their own.*
—JOHANN WOLFGANG VON GOETHE (1749–1832)
GERMAN WRITER

In this lesson, we'll look at foreign words that have made their way into the English language.

AS YOU LEARNED in Lesson 5, a large percentage of English words derive from Latin roots. Latin forms the basis of many languages spoken in the Americas and Europe, a group of languages that is collectively known as the Romance languages. The Romance languages include Spanish, Portuguese, French, Italian, Romanian, and Catalan. Although many of our words are derived from Latin, English is officially considered a Germanic language because of its grammatical structure. If you've ever taken Spanish, French, or Italian, however, you know that Romance and Germanic languages have many similarities.

There are also many English words that come from Greek or other languages. Although all English words were originally derived from other sources, many words have been adopted into the English language directly from other languages without any changes. Usually, we have taken these words because there are no English words that carry the exact same meaning; often these are words used in writing about history or politics—and cooking. Culinary terms such as *paella*, *salsa*, *cabernet*, *chutney*, *croissant*, and *antipasto* come to us unchanged from foreign languages.

Don't shy away from using foreign words in your writing for fear of spelling them incorrectly. If you choose a few select words to learn, you can use them with great impact. That is one reason why words from other languages have found their way into English: they make an impact that an English word simply cannot.

....

TIP: No need to learn the whole language of foreign words that confuse you. Just practice, practice, practice—and commit the spelling of your chosen words to memory. You may benefit from creating mnemonics (described in Lesson 2) for the foreign words that you want to learn to spell. Make your mnemonics personal so they hold meaning; this will make the words easier to remember.

....

COMMONLY USED FOREIGN WORDS

The following table includes 24 commonly used foreign words, their meanings, and some sticky spelling situations that you should watch out for. Use this list as a starting point for developing your own list of high-impact foreign words.

Word	Meaning	Watch Out!
aficionado	person who likes, knows about, and is devoted to a particular activity or thing	only one *f*; tricky *cio* combination
avant-garde	advance group, especially in the visual, literary, or musical arts, whose works are characterized chiefly by unorthodox and experimental methods	hyphenated compound; no *u* in *garde*
blasé	boring as the result of overexposure	accent on the *e*
bourgeois	showing excessive concern for material goods	tricky second syllable: *geois*
cliché	phrase or saying that has been overused and, as a result, has little significance	accent on the *e*

Word	Meaning	Watch Out!
connoisseur	one who knows a lot about a certain subject	double *n* and double *s*; ends with *eur*, not *ure*
debut	first appearance	silent *t*
déjà vu	feeling or sensation that one has been in the exact same situation before	two words; accents on *e* and *a*
élan	distinctive flair or style	starts with an *e*, not an *a*
entrepreneur	person who starts his or her own business	ends with *eur*, not *ure*
epitome	person or thing that is typical of or represents the features of a whole class	ends with *e*, not *y*
façade	false front or face	accent (cedilla) on the *c*
fait accompli	an accomplished, completed deed or act	two words; first is not *fet*
gauche	awkward or crude; lacking in social grace or sensitivity	vowel combination is *au*, not *ow*
imbroglio	misunderstanding or disagreement of a complicated or bitter nature	don't forget the *g*
ingénue	a naïve, innocent young woman or girl, most often in a dramatic production	starts with *i*, not *e*
laissez-faire	policy opposing government control of economic matters except in the case of maintaining peace and the concept of property	hyphenated compound
malaise	feeling of mental unease or discomfort	tricky second syllable: *laise*
naïve	innocent, simple, lacking knowledge of the world	vowel combination is *aï*, not *ai*
non sequitur	statement having no connection to the previous statement or idea	two words, second ends with *ur*, not *our*
passé	out of fashion	double *s*; accent on the *e*

Word	Meaning	Watch Out!
rendezvous	meeting	one word; don't forget the *z*
spiel	talk given for the purpose of luring an audience or selling a product	begins with *sp*; no *h*
vendetta	grudge or feud characterized by acts of retaliation	double *t*

PRACTICE

Identify the foreign words that are spelled correctly in each of the following pairs. Since only some of these have appeared in this lesson, you may want to consult your dictionary for this exercise. Look up the words you don't know, and pay attention to the spelling—and, while you're at it, the meaning.

1. entrapruneur   entrepreneur

2. stanza   stonza

3. shpiel   spiel

4. amigo   amego

5. coux   coup

6. oeuvre   ouver

7. vinyette   vignette

8. ingénue   engénue

9. epitome   apitomee

10. passay   passé

11. au gratin   eau graden

12. dilettante   dillatante

13. callamary   calamari

14. laissay-faire   laissez-faire

15. ciao   chiao

ANSWERS

1. entrepreneur
2. stanza
3. spiel
4. amigo
5. coup
6. oeuvre
7. vignette
8. ingénue
9. epitome
10. passé
11. au gratin
12. dilettante
13. calamari
14. laissez-faire
15. ciao

POSTTEST

NOW THAT YOU HAVE COMPLETED the 30 spelling lessons, it's time to find out what you've learned and how your spelling has improved. The posttest that follows includes 30 questions based on the spelling lessons in this book. You may want to write the answers on a separate sheet of paper so that you can take this test as many times as you'd like.

Check your work when you're done by looking at the answers on pages 209–210.

Write out each word, using hyphens to divide it by its syllables.

1. laughable   _____

2. changing   _____

3. story   _____

4. egocentric   _____

5. February   _____

Write out the correct contractions of the following sets of words.

6. we are   _____

7. would not   _____

8. he will   _____

9. they are   _____

Choose the correct word to complete each sentence.

10. He had been *laying / lying* on the hammock all afternoon.

11. Brady was trying to find an *anecdote / anicdote* to include in his speech.

12. The tight bandage *aggrivated / aggravated* her ankle.

13. The *personal / personnel* office is at the rear of the building.

14. My uncle's office is on the first floor of the *Legislative / legislative* office building.

15. Sarah was often asking whether or not she was *prettier / prettyer* than other girls.

16. The two *restaurants / restaurant's* were across the street from each other.

17. Bailey had *two / too* invitations to the prom.

18. They couldn't *here / hear* the movie well from their seats in the balcony.

19. That was *Lucy's / Lucys* coat, but now it is mine.

20. I think I don't like the *consistency / consistancy* of this cake.

21. *Their / They're* still running laps, even though it is dark out!

22. The new teacher spent the evening reviewing the many *curricula / curriculums* that were available to her.

Correctly spell the plural form of each of the following words.

23. occupant   _____

24. nominee   _____

25. roof   _____

26. moose   _____

27. alumnus   _____

28. man   _____

29. engine   _____

30. buffalo   _____

ANSWERS

1. laugh-a-ble (Lesson 3)
2. chang-ing (Lesson 3)
3. stor-y (Lesson 3)
4. e-go-cen-tric (Lesson 3)
5. Feb-ru-a-ry (Lesson 3)
6. we're (Lesson 16)
7. wouldn't (Lesson 16)
8. he'll (Lesson 16)
9. they're (Lesson 16)
10. He had been *lying* on the hammock all afternoon. (Lesson 27)
11. Brady was trying to find an *anecdote* to include in his speech. (Lesson 11)
12. The tight bandage *aggravated* her ankle. (Lesson 27)
13. The *personnel* office is at the rear of the building. (Lesson 27)

14. My uncle's office is on the first floor of the *legislative* office building. (Lesson 18)

15. Sarah was often asking whether or not she was *prettier* than other girls. (Lesson 22)

16. The two *restaurants* were across the street from each other. (Lesson 20)

17. Bailey had *two* invitations to the prom. (Lesson 25)

18. They couldn't *hear* the movie well from their seats in the balcony. (Lesson 25)

19. That was *Lucy's* coat, but now it is mine. (Lesson 16)

20. I think I don't like the *consistency* of this cake. (Lesson 11)

21. *They're* still running laps, even though it is dark out! (Lesson 25)

22. The new teacher spent the evening reviewing the many *curricula* that were available to her. (Lesson 21)

23. occupants (Lesson 20)

24. nominees (Lesson 20)

25. roofs (Lesson 20)

26. moose (Lesson 21)

27. alumni (Lesson 21)

28. men (Lesson 21)

29. engines (Lesson 20)

30. buffalos (Lesson 20)